SEA

SUMMIT

SEA

SUMMIT

poems

YI LU

Translated from the Chinese and Introduced by
FIONA SZE-LORRAIN

Foreword by MELISSA KWASNY

MILKWEED EDITIONS

Published 2015 by Milkweed Editions
Printed in the United States of America
Cover & book design by Mary Austin Speaker
Cover painting by George Frederik Watts
15 16 17 18 19   5 4 3 2 1
First Edition

Milkweed Editions, an independent nonprofit publisher, gratefully acknowledges sustaining
support from the the Lindquist & Vennum Foundation; the McKnight Foundation; the
National Endowment for the Arts; the Target Foundation; and other generous contributions
from foundations, corporations, and individuals. Also, this activity is made possible by the
voters of Minnesota through a Minnesota State Arts Board Operating Support grant, thanks
to a legislative appropriation from the arts and cultural heritage fund, and a grant from the
Wells Fargo Foundation Minnesota. For a full listing of Milkweed Editions supporters,
please visit www.milkweed.org.

Library of Congress Cataloging-in-Publication Data

Yi, Lu, 1956-
 [Poems. Selections. English]
 Sea summit : poems / Yi Lu ; translated by Fiona Sze-Lorrain. -- First edition.
  pages cm
 ISBN 978-1-57131-476-5 (paperback) -- ISBN 978-1-57131-936-4 (ebook)
 I. Sze-Lorrain, Fiona, translator. II. Title.
 PL2972.5.I36A2 2015
 895.11'52--dc23
                    2015017023

Milkweed Editions is committed to ecological stewardship. We strive to align our book
production practices with this principle, and to reduce the impact of our operations in
the environment. We are a member of the Green Press Initiative, a nonprofit coalition of
publishers, manufacturers, and authors working to protect the world's endangered forests
and conserve natural resources. *Sea Summit* was printed on acid-free 30% postconsumer-
waste paper by Versa Press.

acknowledgments

Grateful acknowledgment to the editors of these magazines in which several of these poems/translations have first appeared: *The Antigonish Review, Asymptote, The Bitter Oleander, The Brooklyn Rail (InTranslation), Cerise Press, Copper Nickel, The Los Angeles Review, Mānoa, Modern Poetry in Translation, Poetry London, Poetry Salzburg Review, Salamander, Upstairs at Duroc, Vallum,* and *World Literature Today.*

Five poems and translations were also published in a hand-bound chapbook *Volcanic Stone* (The Offending Adam, 2012).

The translator wishes to thank Sally Molini, Susan Thomas, Mark Strand, Christina Cook, Wayne Miller, and Melissa Kwasny.

contents

II

III

IV

V

This winter, the flocks of redpolls have arrived again on the snow-crusted prairie near my home here in Montana. Finch-like, cheerful, with a pink wash on their pale breasts, they are an irruptive species, meaning that they migrate irregularly from their summer in the Arctic tundra and that there is no predicting what year they will arrive. Their lives and their patterns are a mystery, their arrival completely unsuspected, quickening my vision of the largeness of the world and how many secrets are still hidden from us. In such a way, Yi Lu's poems of sea force and mountain force have come to me, from across the Atlantic Ocean, via Fiona Sze-Lorrain, Yi's sensitive translator in Paris, and from across central Europe, from her home in Fuzhou, the Chinese southern coastal city where she lives. And, although her language and life are unfamiliar to me, I feel touched by something unpredicted and bright, with power to change and enlarge me.

Given that most of Yi's poetry is set out of doors—amid birdsong, butterflies, rain, and wind—it is tempting to place her work within the tradition of classical Chinese poetry with its precise imagery and symbolic connections between the natural and the human. One quick look through the table of contents reveals poems entitled "Early Spring," "March Pasture," "A Pregnant Woman Walks in the Fields," and "Goats on a Desert Island," poetry seemingly of the pastoral, set in a more innocent time, without acid rain or traffic or fracking. Yet in this work there is indeed a sense of contemporary unease between the speaker and the nonhuman forces of nature, as well as a sense of peril, that might also be placed under the contemporary rubric of "ecopoetry" or the "postmodern pastoral," as defined in several recent American books and anthologies I have been reading. Although one might argue that all poetry speaks to this subject matter—ecology being the study of organisms and the environment in which they live—in ecopoetry, there is an emphasis both on our current state of ecological crisis and our complicated history and relationship to nature.

One need only look at the first poem in *Sea Summit*, entitled "Early Spring," to see many of these concerns addressed. The poem begins with the vivid image of four cow tails swishing above the tall grass of a meadow, seemingly disconnected from their bodies, a typical pastoral image: placeless, timeless, benign. Immediately, though, it is clear that this is not simply a "nature poem," in the sense of attempting to describe something beautiful in nature, what Joshua Corey, in his introduction to the anthology *The Arcadia Project: North American Postmodern Pastoral*, calls "the mediated dreamscape of images passively consumed." Although the image is described in traditional figurative language—the swishing is "as solemn as a congealed storm"—the image is odd, inauspicious, initiating in the poet an unexpected response: "their bowed heads seem unrelated to their tails / each cow also seems unrelated to itself / is the grass it eats also unrelated to its stomach." We are often, of course, like the cow, unrelated to our own bodies or what we put into them. But there is more. No longer timeless, the poem is set in early spring, in the very instant before its irruption, when even the changing of the season—the clocklike rhythm of the tails—is on hold, as if it were no longer guaranteed: "even the butterfly seems unrelated to itself."

Here we have the opposite of the clichés of ecology, of everything harmoniously interrelating with everything else. What about those moments when there is no harmony? When we are in conflict? When we fight each other? Yi's is a fearless, momentary, new perspective, the world alienated even from itself. The next poem, "March Pasture," begins with the speaker questioning her own role in this instability: "did I block the surging moisture / or mess up the barely stable order / the world struggles to arrange / its immensity / standing in the pasture isn't relaxing in March." The shepherd in the traditional pastoral, standing in the pasture, king of his flocks, is here undermined by anxiety. Did her mere presence (did ours?) destabilize the essential stability of the seasons or of the climate or of history? "[A] butterfly that comes too soon stumbles like a drunk": is this an image of global warming, or is it the comment of someone whose doctrinaire understanding of the world is falling apart? *Whose* authority can claim it is too soon?

In *Sea Summit*, we are invited not into a world but in relation to the world. The poet is embedded as human and female and responsible and responsive. A treeful of bird calls disrupts her: "like starlight like scissors like nails." She feels the trembling of a bud about to burst open, the tremendous effort and fragility involved. "What baffled me," she writes, "was the unusual ties / between a mother and the sun." We used to call sensibility like this clairvoyant—the ability to see clearly into the distance, whether temporal or spatial. Yi sees through as well as is seen through:

> behind the hill comes the first wind
> pushing open a small window in my chest
> then   more winds from the jarrah trees   the rapeflower field
> all in a rush
> my well-sealed body   can hardly stay shut

One might call this point of view one of "multisubjectivity." René Char, the great French visionary poet, would no doubt name Yi one of his "Transparents."

These poems are not records detailing the "passive consumption of images" but active encounters with the Image itself. For Yi, the sun, moon, and clouds are personages requiring the attention and extreme listening that any stranger or beloved might. "I see a huge solitude," she writes, "like a giant at the end of the road." It is this presence that one senses immediately in her poems, a solitude so much bigger than herself that she finds herself "like a little child / wheeling toward it." The canyon, the valley, the heavy rain are not metaphors in her poems but the roots of metaphor, irreducible to anything but pure being. Yi enters the "gigantic network" of nature, the "rowdy conference room" of the sea summit, and they, in turn, pass through her, resulting in poems of particular intensity, mystery, and transaction. This is the visionary potential of ecopoetry: a practice that invites the presence of wind, butterfly, storm to meet and disrupt us, just as they disrupt and interrupt each other and the rest of the world. It is a practice, both interior and exterior, irruptive as well as interruptive. As Tom Cheetham writes in *All the World an Icon*, his meditation on Sufi scholar Henry Corbin and the use of image as spiritual practice, "We are changed utterly, ontologically: in our very being, by the exercise of the Active Imagination—and this allows us to see things that we otherwise cannot see." This is also what poetry like Yi's can precipitate in us.

MELISSA KWASNY

Behind the Isle—
Translating Yi Lu

While the tradition of pastoral poetry continues to be practiced in the West, few contemporary Chinese poets have grounded the corpus of their work and aesthetics in ecopoetics. In fact, ecocritical attention is scant. This is hardly a surprise, given the dominance of a Marxist ideology in favor of harnessing nature. Born in 1956 in Fujian province of southern China, Yi Lu[1] started publishing her work in the eighties. Beyond the one-paragraph biography included here, not much is known about her life. She stands as a voice of her own, associated with neither a movement nor school of thought—certainly not under the flagship of political endorsement. This is no easy task, considering the context of a Communist state whose history and culture are engendered by Confucian ethics, Maoist discourse, and collective consciousness. Over the years, Yi's work has steadily found its readership because of consistency and an engagement with ecology through language. Thoreau wrote, "We need the tonic of wildness . . . as [a] farm does loads of muck." In taking this angle, Yi deviates from those who adopt a rhetoric based on Utilitarianism. She commits herself to poetry as the spiritual medium between language, nature, and science—a shifting paradigm that reconnects humanity with nature, this in spite of failures and tension in the inhabited time, space, imagination, or vision.

---

1   Yi is the poet's family name. Most Chinese names consist of three characters or syllables. In this case, the poet goes by Yi Lu—with the surname preceding her first name, Lu—as her given name has only one character or syllable.

"An ecopoem," as Nebraska-based James Engelhardt champions in a manifesto for ecopoetry, "might play with slippages, but the play will lead to further connections."[2] This offers a useful lens for reading Yi Lu, who in a preface for her award-winning volume, *See* (2004), provides a similar perspective of her oeuvre: "There are many things we can't see. Not because they have yet to appear, but that we have not visibly connected with them." To connect, to return—this is how she envisions a responsible life, a cognitive mind, as one that perceives the world, not as one that explains it. The linguistic effort to reach this intactness is a process of intimacy, mindful of the nonhuman, listening to silence. Ultimately, it seeks unity— to be *in*, *with*, and *of* an ever-evolving organic experience:

> touching its grass and trees   and petals
> my heart sways   a boat has left my body
> but why should I drift with the tide
> what relates me to this raft this water
> what links me with behind the isle
> what will unite at last
> —"Behind the Isle," p. 49

Currently a resident in urban Fuzhou, the capital city of Fujian, Yi Lu is nostalgic for the sea and mountains: they incarnate specific landscapes and emotions that accompanied her during her childhood and through her young adulthood. When asked, in an interview, about her poetic origins, she vaguely recalls her teenage years during the Cultural Revolution[3] (1966-

---

2   This critical piece, "The Language Habitat: An Ecopoetry Manifesto" by James Engelhardt, appeared in the online poetry magazine *Octopus*, Issue 9.

3   During the Cultural Revolution, Yi Lu's father was demoted from his

1976), and though her first poem was lost, it had "something to do with the sea." She continued, "I saw in some children's books beautiful illustrations of the sea, with clouds and in an azure blue, that looked totally different from those existing in my reality. I was probably inspired to write my 'first' poem because of this poignant longing for such clouds and sea."[4] Much has been written on how poets live and relive their childhood through poetry, but Yi's account in this case informs us more about the recurring relevance of the sea in the poet's work; it is as if the sea had defined her poetic vocation before she herself realized it. The title of the poem, "Sea First Man Next" is a self-explanatory allusion. In another, "No Prop Can Shield You," the elusive *you* erases the personification of the sea, only to reinsert the "you" and the "sea" back into the theater of imagination to dramatic effects:

> you are a prop
> used for contrast   perception
> people relax   free   or in a heavier daze
> now   you are a stirring wound   an eye full of tears
> no prop can shield you
>
> in the walls of a city
> thinking of you naked and far in the dark
> I'll stay awake with you   this instant and next
> divided by the tossing and turning of an abyss
> —"No Prop Can Shield You," p. 69

governmental post and sent to the country for "re-education." Yi spent her childhood in a village near "a gray, sinister sea."

4   From an unpublished interview with the translator (November 3, 2011).

Here, the reversibility of "you"—from sea to a spectator (or the immediate reader?), then back to "I" the narrator/poet—is achieved without metaphor. The sea the poem, the poem the poet. The sea is for Yi Lu what the "Image" is for Ezra Pound: one that "presents an intellectual and emotional complex in an instant of time," its "presentation" the release of "that sense of sudden liberation; that sense of freedom from time limits and space limits; that sense of sudden growth, which we experience in the presence of the greatest works of art."[5] More narrative-driven "sea monologues" include "Drift Bottle," "Many Many Mothers," "My Own Sea," "Using Two Seas," and "A Dog on the Shore," which are found in the second section of this bilingual collection. Even the book title *Sea Summit*, chosen by Yi, is a symbolic gesture.

By extension, virtually all her poems here carry a statement on, or illustration of, nature. Such is her call to arms for an aesthetic to reflect this identity—not by deference, but of belonging—the transcendence of a mortal existence in this universe. But Yi Lu is a reticent artist; to see Yi as a spokesperson for ecological causes undercuts the lyrical vitality of the poems. For her, writing functions more as an experience of feeling *chez soi* than the endeavor of creating another home. In her work, you can read patience: a gentle ritual of each verse peeling an image away, moment by moment—as slow as possible but with surprising turns. Even the gentlest poem has its rigor: it controls its forward momentum. The most unforgettable ones are often hesitant to settle for emotional resolution by a clean stroke. Also, the speaker in these poems elucidates moral truth with tenderness. I like this ethics: the poet takes care of the reader.

---

5   Pound, Ezra. "A Retrospect." *Literary Essays of Ezra Pound*. Ed. T.S. Eliot. New York: New Directions, 1968. 4.

Yi Lu is a theater scenographer and set designer by profession. The challenge for a scenographer is the interpretation of space, *creating suggestive space and linking space with dramatic time.*[6] As stage designer, she is ranked "national first-level." She is also a painter. Naturally, colors and visual form offer immediate choices that help her to *visually liberate the text.*[7] She thinks of geometry as a measure of mood. Without sentimentalism, or extravagant verbalism, her work speaks, in an image-driven language, to the transience of matter. I consider Yi Lu a quiet poet who says something "shapeful," yet precise. To question the role of a (post-)modern human existence in a larger cosmos, she evokes and invokes nature in its grandeur or small moments, but with a philosophically inquiring mind. The agenda does not stop at celebration:

> the world has many lakes
> some frozen   some boiling at a volcano's peak
> some saltier than seawater
> most fresh and cool, green and pleasing
>
> stillness is self weighing on self
> many things controlled unwittingly
> —"Lake, Again," p. 179

Birds and trees populate Yi Lu's imagination, as she writes and creates art from her study with a window facing a sturdy tree. A curious observer of the tree's "bird visitors," Yi wakes up to their call, and begins

---

6   Howard, Pamela. *What Is Scenography?* London: Routledge, 2002. 1.

7   "The scenographer visually liberates the text and the story behind it, by creating a world in which the eyes see what the ears do not hear." *Ibid*, 33.

her day with a sense of awe. What is profundity but the gestation of *listen*? She waits for birds and the tree to speak to her. The act in its essence is a proof of faith. To chronicle surprises that birds bring her in the day is the extension of this ritual witnessing of the nonhuman. The experience is both restorative and sacred, short of permanence but filled with effort:

> a treeful of bird calls like starlight   like scissors   like nails
> [. . .]
>
> in my body rooms emerge one by one
> one by one rooms emerge with bells
>
> I'm like a treeful of bird calls
> wake up   dress   exercise   freshen up
> I jingle like a treeful of bird calls
>
> light   and expand my rooms one by one
> like a treeful of bird calls I'm fully lit   ready to work
> —"A Treeful of Bird Calls," p. 29

Literary critics in China make frequent reference to Yi Lu's word-by-word elegance, and how it runs in counterpoint with a theatrical texture. Within a poem, these two trademarks play a role in molding an architecture—both visual and formal—that is distinctly hers. Asymmetrical yet with a natural poise, her verses expand lyrical possibilities while keeping intact the density of a personal narrative. Words in a verse behave like notes, each with a sound before coming together as a string of meanings. Cadence, or movement, pulls and pushes each line, creating a playfulness between space and verse. The impact of a trompe-l'œil is accentuated when the writing tames itself into a miniature visual artwork. And it becomes what we may recognize as a calligram or a word-shaped poem:

> bird calls play on the mountainside
> tug at clouds
> widen the coil of light
> crack it
> transfigure it
> avoid neatness

> bird calls guide the way for the lazy slow spring
> > like a flight of stairs they fall
> > > like a flight of stairs they fall
> > > > like a flight of stairs they fall
> —"Bird Call on a Spring Day," p. 121

Overall, Yi Lu communicates from a bodied relation to sound and image. Conscious of how the spatial arrangement of words on a page may affect their sonic effect, she believes disparate words in a poem have a greater need for independence than musical notes in terms of implications.[8] Punctuation free, the poems generate a different dynamic that encourages more choices in diction. A pause or a sound is at once detail and event. In lieu of commas or periods, she substitutes indent spacings, each resembling an empty space on the stage. Words become the actors. In turn, volatility is introduced; as a juncture between ideas or temporality, blank spacings embody the potential of enjambments,

---

8   From an unpublished interview with the translator (November 3, 2011).

interruptives, and disjunctions. Emptiness is responsive in this internal jazz that externalizes the leap from one image to another. I cannot resist the thought of such aesthetics pledging allegiance to the poet's cross-disciplinary practice in theater, dramaturgy, and set design. The opening stanza of "Space of Drama" is particularly resonant:

word   phrase   period—
a mountain stream   a lofty mountain range   a monastery
from far to near
abyss hangs in mid-sky   visible in all directions
a wave   kowtows before the ocean
mountain peaks buried under the sea
—"Space of Drama," p. 197

During the translation of *Sea Summit*, I found some help from an observation by American poet Jane Hirshfield:

A person's heard voice is replete with information. So it is with the voice of a poem, directing us in myriad ways into the realm it inhabits—a realm more or less formal, more or less argumentative, more or less emotional, linear, textured. As we gauge a person's kindness by tone, regardless of what she is saying, we similarly recognize a poem's tenderness or harshness toward the world around it; its engagement or detachment . . . [9]

Inspired to locate the tone, and to follow the breath of the thought behind each verse, I thus asked Yi Lu to read the poems aloud during our weekly

---

9   Hirshfield, Jane. "Poetry and the Mind of Concentration." *Nine Gates: Entering the Mind of Poetry*. New York: HarperCollins Publishers, 1998. 29.

Skype meetings. There are instances of quiet, defense, surrender, and anticipation, all of which seek translation and to be determined by the intensity of listening. However, I am reluctant to focus on the process of translation—its worthy accidents, defeats, and investigations—instead of the poetry and its ecological literacy. This might have something to do with a moral impulse from an era when our children must confront industrial toxins in their daily life. At the same time, astute citizens might grow conscious of a political and cultural "trendiness" to ecological concerns in America or Europe today. It makes me anxious to think of us reading Yi Lu simply as a departure point for discussions on ecopoetics. To introduce her as first a poet, next a woman poet, then a lyrical poet and an "eco-poet" is thus less an attempt at seeking a singular audience than an experiment to transport these "labels" to another culture or reality. What does it mean to have a poet—a woman, a mother, in a country of more than 1.3 billion—address our increasingly catastrophic attitudes toward nature and its imbalance, and to do so in China's difficult and politically determined culture? What does it signify for China and the rest of the world?

Sea Summit compiles Yi Lu's work over a span of more than two decades. It includes poems from four of her five volumes. While Yi Lu began publishing her writings in 1984, her debut collection, *On the Cusp of Youth*, appeared only in 1991. The second, *Voyage*, was published by the national press in Beijing, The Writers' Publishing House, in 1997. It took another seven years before a third book, *See* (2004), materialized. The union of nature and symbolic vision—what Yi Lu defines as "the unseen limit"—is a thematic concern in *See* as well as *Using Two Seas* (2009). Her fifth volume, *Forever Lingering* (2011), contains new sequenced poems that evolve from earlier narratives in *See*. As I write, I think of Rilke: "The great poetry begins in elegy and ends in praise." *Sea Summit* begins in elegiac speculation—"even the butterfly seems unrelated to itself"—and ends with a wish, *May you see the splendor of stars in this world*. It is not the cliché but a sense of awakening that this language of praise creates.

FIONA SZE-LORRAIN

I

早春

忽然发现整片原野唯一在动的是
　　四只牛的尾巴
庄重如凝着风暴
一撩一拨都似叮咛
牛低沉的头仿佛和身后的尾巴无关
牛也仿佛与自己无关
被它啃进的青草是否也和肠胃无关
四条拂天拍地的尾巴间
多了一只翻山越谷的蝴蝶
这蝴蝶也仿佛与它自己无关

Early Spring

suddenly I found the only stirring in the fields
    the tails of four cows
as solemn as a congealed storm
its swish and sway like an urge
their bowed heads seem unrelated to their tails
each cow also seems unrelated to itself
is the grass it eats also unrelated to its stomach
between their four whisking tails
a butterfly waltzes over hill and dale
even the butterfly seems unrelated to itself

三月的原野

我是否阻碍了涌动的湿气
弄乱了好不容易稳住的秩序
大地在安排广大无边的力
困难重重
站在三月的原野一点也轻松不起来

一朵花苞绽开一点　　又绽开一点
我想扶住花茎　　使它不要颤抖
那细弱的喘息联向苍穹

一只过早出现的蝴蝶像踉跄而至的醉汉
我一挥手它就颠三倒四无踪影
却无法喝住乱蹿而过的小风

浓稠的阳光仿佛直接灌进爱里
三月的原野
茫茫拔高的是壮烈的心血
好像整条河里流的都是眼泪

March Pasture

did I block the surging moisture
or mess up the barely stable order
the world struggles to arrange
its immensity
standing in the pasture isn't relaxing in March

a bud bursts open   little by little
I want to hold the stem   so it won't tremble
a thin feeble gasping links to the sky

a butterfly that comes too soon stumbles like a drunk
I wave my hand   it turns upside down and disappears
but I can't stop the wind trampling all over

creamy sunlight seems to pour itself into love
March pasture
heroic pains at vast heights
as if the whole river was flowing with tears

孕妇在田野上走

她的身体太满了
一路泼溅——
大团的云朵和花群

溪水顺着她粗壮的双腿爬上去
像去补充一座大湖

她一路摇摇晃晃
都有风和阳光扶着

她裙摆的阴影像巨大的黑蝶
要赶走那些生动的小草

她的目光茫茫　抹杀了所有障碍
大山也隆重地移开

她要和一棵桂树并排走
桂树又怎能不答应呢

但她想从这田野　分离出来
就不容易了

A Pregnant Woman Walks in the Fields

her body is too full
spilling over all the way—
fat lumps of clouds and flowers

stream water climbs up her bulky legs
like replenishing a big lake

lifted by wind and light
she wavers all the way

like a huge black butterfly the shadow of her skirt
wants to chase away small vivid grass

her vast gaze   wipes away obstacles
even the mountain shifts solemnly

she wants to walk with a cinnamon tree
how can the cinnamon tree disagree

but to split herself   from these fields
isn't easy

鸟叫

一声鸟叫
裂花一样
一声这样近的鸟叫
心痛一样
使我像一声鸟叫一样惊起

我像一声鸟叫一样在房间里回旋
像一声鸟叫一样扑向窗口

窗外一声　两声　三声的鸟叫看着我
第四声鸟叫已在很远的山边……

Bird Call

a bird call
like a shattered flower
a bird call so near
like heartache
leaving me panicked like a bird call

I spin in the room like a bird call
dashing to the window like a bird call

outside the window one   two   three bird calls look at me
the fourth is already far by the mountain . . .

呼喊

是电话出了故障
母亲忽然听不到我的声音
可我仍能听见她的
听见母亲对着话筒惊惶地喊我的名字
就像小时候对着旷野喊我
就像以为我丢了
再也叫不应了
我感到耳膜被拂过很多山冈的北风撞击
终于听见壳啦一声
母亲那边寂然无声了　　音讯全无了
这回轮到我呼喊了
妈妈……妈妈啊……

Yell

something must be wrong with the phone
Mother suddenly can't hear me
but I can still hear her
hearing her panic and yell my name into the phone
like yelling for me in the wild when I was little
thinking I was lost
and would never respond
my eardrums feel the hit of a north wind from many hills
at last a click
silence on Mother's end   not a sound
now it's my turn to yell
Mother... O Mother...

篮子里的父亲

妹妹在电话中说
她和姐姐把父亲的骨灰盒
放在一个篮子里
提着到山中　置进一个
单元住宅般的公墓里

正被手头的工作
压得胸口发闷的我
想象那个篮子
摇摇晃晃的
登着石阶　绕过山弯
前前后后　草气花香
里面的父亲　就变成
一窝鸟卵　一罐泉水　几粒乌饭果

记起以前的父亲
曾对我说
多么想闲下来
写写毛笔字
但总有那么多事要忙
家里也没有个合适的地方

Father in a Basket

on the phone my sister said
she and elder sister put Father's urn
in a basket
carried up a mountain   placed
in a cemetery resembling apartments

work stress at hand
pressing my chest
I imagine the basket
swaying
taking stone steps   around a mountain bend
back and forth   grass and floral scent
Father inside   becomes
a nest of eggs   a jar of spring water   a few blueberries

I remember Father
once said
how he wished to slow down
and enjoy calligraphy
yet he was always so busy
without a good place at home to practice

一树的鸟鸣

一树的鸟鸣像星光　像剪刀　像钉子
像阶梯　像一小段一小段的河流
一树的鸟鸣像一座忙碌的锻造厂

我的身体里有了一个又一个的房间
一个又一个的房间里挂着铃子

我像一树鸟鸣一样
起床　穿衣　晨练　梳洗
我像一树鸟鸣一样叮叮当当

把自己的一个一个房间叫亮　叫宽敞
我像一树鸟鸣一样通体光明　开始上班

A Treeful of Bird Calls

a treeful of bird calls like starlight   like scissors   like nails
like ladders   like a river passage by passage
a treeful of bird calls like a hectic forge

in my body rooms emerge one by one
one by one rooms emerge with bells

I'm like a treeful of bird calls
wake up   dress   exercise   freshen up
I jingle like a treeful of bird calls

light   and expand my rooms one by one
like a treeful of bird calls I'm fully lit   ready to work

花朵

它怎么知道这样的瓣形会和其它的花朵不一样
怎么知道花蕊要旋成小水潭的模样才更显得沉静含蓄
怎么知道花色从瓣根向瓣沿由浅至深洇染才更显层次丰富
怎么知道香气要来路不明　要不可想像
才能从众多花香里区别出来　而不至于混淆
花朵没有雕刻刀　调色盘　化妆盒
花朵是怎样创造自己的
除了我们知道的阳光　雨露和春风还有什么在帮助花朵
那些有韵致的　个性化的　智慧的部分来源于什么
遥远的　不为我们所知的餐桌上有没有花朵灵感的胃囊
在我们看来空无一物的空气里有没有花朵的宝镜　纤手和学堂
世界上若有事物比花朵更懂得美丽
花朵会不会自责和害羞
花朵怎么知道自己是花朵呢

Flower

how does it know this petal shape will differ from other flowers
know that pistil must spiral like a pond for a look more placid and
    reserved
know that color darkens from petal end to rim for a look more
    layered and richer
know that fragrance must come from nowhere   unimagined
in order to stand out among flowers   not to be mixed
the flower has no carving knife   color palette   cosmetics kit
how does the flower invent itself
other than sunlight   rain and dew and spring wind   who else is
    helping the flower
what do those graceful   unique   intelligent parts stem from
afar   is there its gastric pouch of inspiration on an unknown meal table
in our bare air its magic mirror   slight hands and classroom
were there things in this world which knew beauty better than the flower
would the flower blame itself and turn shy
how does the flower know it is a flower

荒岛上的羊

一个荒岛
上面有几只无人照看的羊
吃野草　喝天水
晚上睡在石洞里

听着这些话的时候
窗外秋阳很暖
屋内却有点冷　我想
那些羊此刻是在秋阳里的
秋阳是像养植物一样养着它们的

那些羊的幸福　肯定是在
描绘所有幸福之词出现之前的幸福
它们的安宁　肯定是在
形容所有安宁之词出现之前的安宁
它们的单纯　一定也是在
表现所有单纯之词出现之前的单纯

我于是就仿佛看见——
它们被风吹得像团团转的菊花似的样子
它们跑到海的跟前也知道害怕似的退回来的样子
它们瞪着翻滚不停的白浪目不转睛的样子

Goats on a Desert Island

on a desert island
some untended goats
eat wild grass   drink sky water
sleep in stone caves at night

when I learn about it
the autumn sun outside feels so warm
but it feels chilly inside   I gather
those goats are now in the autumn sun
which nurtures them like plants

those goats' happiness   must be
happiness beyond depiction
their peace   must be
peace beyond description
their innocence   must also be
innocence beyond expression

and I imagine—
how they are blown by wind like swirling chrysanthemums
how they run to the sea and shrink in fear
how they stare at white waves that toss and turn

小时候去外婆家

小时候去外婆家
绕过两个山弯
穿过一片田地
沿着河边走一阵
再过一道石桥
……
那时的我才一点点大
看见羊的时候停一停
看见鹅的时候停一停
看见蝴蝶又停一停
那时候没听说有恶棍会拐小孩
整片山野只有我一个人

On My Way to Grandma When I Was Little

on my way to Grandma when I was little
I'd go round two mountain curves
cross a field
walk along a river
over a stone bridge
. . .
I was so little then
seeing a goat I'd stop
seeing a goose I'd stop
seeing a butterfly I'd stop again
back then no one heard of stealing children
there was only me on the whole mountain

桂花的清香

桂花的清香
停在烟尘之中
仿佛不经意的提醒

一路上若隐若现
不屈不挠地跟随
细细的针尖
拨弄我的心眼
有清泉涌出　渗开

以至我不舍得拐进
　　回家的弄堂
就这样和它
去了很多美丽深情的地方
感谢世界总让我多幸福一点

Sweet Olive Scent

sweet olive scent
hangs in smoke and dust
like a casual reminder

elusive all the way
trailing tirelessly
fine needle tips
prick my heart
clear spring water flows   oozing out

till I can't bear to make a turn
    for the alley home
accompanying it just like this
to many beautiful and tender places
thankful that the world blesses me a little more

春天的茶花

茶花的蕾像小小的坚硬的乳房似的
像欲爆的小炸弹似的
满树的嘟着鲜红嘴唇的茶花的蕾
一看就知道很任性

确实已经绷得快裂开了
那绿色的夹袄一开始就该做大一点
春天的布料总是不够用的

花树已显出透支的倦容
很早我就担心它会管不动那么多花的
它的决心那么大
好像还有周密的计划

但春天里一切都无法按部就班
南风来的时候万物都会昏厥一阵
那本来比金盏菊迟开的蛱蝶花
昨夜不知怎的就憋不住了

比婚礼的百褶裙还要繁复的茶花
　　是很重的
并不强壮的花树快跪下来了
大地知道不知道呢
车水马龙　气喘吁吁的大地啊
茶花旁边还有三棵喳喳叫嚷着开放的
　　栀子花

Spring Camellias

camellia buds like tiny steely breasts
tiny bombs about to explode
treeful of buds pouting with fresh red lips
so willful at a glance

stretched until about to crack
that green-padded jacket should be made bigger
spring fabric is never enough

the flower tree unveils its overfatigue
I've long worried it can't take care of so many flowers
its determination
with thorough plans to come

but spring can't follow its own prescribed order
the world faints lightly upon the south wind
peacock flowers should bloom after marigolds
oddly last night they could wait no more

more intricate than pleated wedding robes
      camellias are very heavy
far from being sturdy the flower tree is almost on its knees
does the earth know
a hectic traffic   O panting earth
next to the camellias three chatty gardenias
      are wailing to bloom

山谷的绿

那山谷是一个大染缸
我只站在它的边上
就觉得有浓郁的绿
从脚底　足尖　指尖渗进来
一下子就遍及全身
心脏也从里面绿出芽来
那些昆虫们肯定都绿透了
连声音都如翡翠片
只有花朵染不进去
它们全都像小碟　小碗　小杯子
满满地盛着自己的颜色

Valley's Green

that valley is a huge dye vat
I just stand on its edge
feel its rich green
oozing from the sole   to toetips   and fingertips
throughout the whole body in an instant
even the heart is sprouting with green
those insects must be green throughout
even voices are like jade pieces
only flowers can't be dyed
all of them like tiny saucers   little bowls   little cups
filled to the brim with their own colors

湛蓝的一小泓

没有溪涧和瀑流
仅在山弯的凹处
渗出湛蓝的一小泓
像一面透视的小镜
使我看到内部的罅隙
曲折的暗道和深宫
看到滴水穿石
深渊下的深渊　湖上的湖
梯台错落　没有天窗
我看到一座山的骨架
所撑持住的一切
看到一座山的隐忍

An Expanse of Azure

no stream no waterfall
just an expanse of azure
oozing from a cavity in a meander
like a tiny transparent mirror
letting me see the internal cracks
through meandering dark tunnels and deep palaces
I see a water drop penetrate a stone
an abyss under the abyss   a lake on the lake
jumbling stairways   no skylight
I see the skeleton of a mountain
upholding everything
see the silent endurance of a mountain

在峡谷里

被雄峰围护的峡谷
随处可见散漫和任性
纷乱的花香　纷乱的落叶
纷乱的阳光　纷乱的风
蓬蓬丛丛的寂静恣肆地叫
荫影里绿紫的血脉奔突着呐喊
迷狂的蝴蝶就要感染镇定的蜻蜓
蜥蜴背上那高耸的孤独碰着大树的枝条取乐
一条野溪拿灵魂一路玩耍

尘世的闹街是因为有暗中的纠纷和抢夺
自然啊你在哪里运筹帷幄

能否也怂恿我一次
没有人会看见我在峡谷里的样子
我的头发散开　双臂舒张
像疯奔的野物
但被那哈哈笑的瀑布淋湿以后
仍不能像近旁的榛树
抖一抖身体就算

In the Canyon

canyon protected by majestic peaks
slackness and willfulness seen everywhere
a whirlpool of floral scent   a whirlpool of falling leaves
a whirlpool of sunlight   a whirlpool of wind
stillness in thick clusters cries without restraint
purple-green blood vessels rush and shout out from the shade
mad butterflies will arouse calm dragonflies
solitude towering on a lizard's back toys with a tree branch
a wild creek plays with the soul all the way

noisy worldly streets of dark disputes and looting
O nature, where are you devising your strategies

can you entice me just once
no one will see how I look in the canyon
my hair set loose   arms stretched wide
like a wild beast running madly
though soaked by a laughing waterfall
I still can't shake it off
like the hazel tree nearby

将逝之物

那年　在一个偏僻的山弯
我看着一树白花
一朵一朵掉落
大山静静的
别的树也静静的
没有去打扰那棵树正在做着的事情

花朵在离开花托那一刻
是有风轻轻推一下的
有时候风的手势不对
那朵花就倾斜在花托上
粘稠的花液被拉得很细
将逝之物　多么被动
一点力气也没有

整座山谷像知道总会发生之事一样
慈宁地等待着
几只夹蝶如不懂事的孩子
闪过来闪过去
倒更像一小片一小片的灵魂

忽有一阵大一点的风带着阳光的金铂
　　撒了过来
整棵花树颤抖起来
我和山谷都觉得太早太仓促了点

Fading Things

that year   at a distant mountain curve
I saw a treeful of white flowers
falter one by one
the mountain kept still
other trees too
left that tree alone

the moment a flower left its calyx
a wind pushed it lightly
sometimes the wind made a wrong move
the flower would lean against its calyx
its milky fluid stretched finely
fading things   so passive
and frail

the valley seemed aware of what loomed ahead
and waited with quiet compassion
like ignorant children butterflies
flashed here and there
didn't they look more like pieces of soul

voilà a stronger wind with gold foils of light
      splashing over
the flower tree shook
the valley and I thought it came *too soon too rushed*

那小岛后面

那小岛后面是什么样子
我们的竹排没有经过那里
那里的水是什么颜色
水流的波纹　岸影　怎样传递消息
有什么样的树丛　什么样的花
歇过什么样的蝴蝶
它们在阳光下怎样呼吸
夜晚　暴风雨　酷暑
会有什么样的事迹

那小岛后面也许我今生无缘亲临
有一阵风吹到我脸上　它们先经过了那里
碰过那里的草木　花瓣
我的心为之摇动　有一只船已离开我的身体
但我为什么要随波逐流
这一方竹排和这一片水域和我是什么关系
那小岛后面与我又有何牵连
哪些东西最终会在一起

Behind the Isle

what is it like behind the isle
our bamboo raft didn't pass by there
what is the color of its water
ripples   shore shadow   how do they carry news
what grove   what flowers
what butterflies have rested there
how do they breathe in the sun
at night   in a storm   in high summer
what will take place

I may never go there in this life
a wind blows against my face   winds were once there
touching its grass and trees   and petals
my heart sways   a boat has left my body
but why should I drift with the tide
what relates me to this raft this water
what links me with behind the isle
what will unite at last

海中的山峰

在喧嚣的会议室里
想着海中的山峰——

波浪正在喧闹
海中的山峰
在离海面多深的地方
四周是否已经寂静

海底的寂静有多么大
海中的山峰把多么大的寂静听进石头里

无序的风仍在海面吹卷
变幻的天色杂染纷乱的水花
但海的身体在寂静里
海中的山峰是埋在寂静里的钉子

看风景的人看不到海中的山峰
除非他能看穿海

或许有被封死的缝隙包藏云朵和星星
或许把紧密的折层摊开也有繁华的斑迹
海中的山峰
用了多少记忆换来忘记

海中的山峰
在离我多远的地方

Sea Summit

in a rowdy conference room
I think of the sea summit—

waves are howling
sea summit
so deep down from the sea's surface
is there already silence all around

how immense the silence an ocean deep
sea summit listens in its rocks to how immense a silence

a chaotic wind swirls on the sea's surface
fluctuating sky colors taint the disheveled sea foam
yet the sea body is inside stillness
its summit buried in the pin of stillness

scenery viewer can't see the sea summit
unless he sees through the sea

clouds and stars may hide in sealed cracks
spots flourish in a spread of delicate folds
sea summit
how many memories does it use to forget

sea summit
in a place so far from me

先有海　后有人

力竭的生灵
辽阔的衣襟抓在谁的手里
如此巨大之躯的扭动
竟没有惊动一颗星粒
要毁灭多少洁白的花

泉流到河里
河流到海里
海能去哪里
深渊就这样形成

当你被一盏台灯定位
远方的海以黑暗延伸你
没有更亮的光能把你围困

一次又一次涌来的白花
决心开放到世界没日的白花
你心里还有什么角落没被铺满

先有海　后有人
这是造物对人类的关怀
海是设置在地球上的行为艺术
一个辽阔的间离

Sea First Man Next

a weary creature
a broad jacket grasped in whose hand
such a huge twist
startles not a grain of star
many white flowers to destroy

springs flow into a river
rivers into the sea
where can the sea go
this is how an abyss is shaped

when a lamp fixes you in space
the distant sea stretches you with darkness
no brighter light can besiege you

white flowers surge on and on
driven to blossom until doom
is there a corner in your heart not coated to its brim

sea first   man next
this is how the Creator cares for man
the sea is a performance art on Earth
a vast distancing

漂流瓶

海上的一个叹号
波浪和风都要在那里停留
总有小小白花护送

是哪一只手
在怎样的时刻
向苍海
交付一个重托

波涛上漂流的心啊
比一尾鱼更没有自持的力量
是否也是一个汪洋
被最后的意志封住出口

使一个胸腔空了
宇宙多了一缕牵挂
地球要怎样旋转
才有一场相遇

结局被谁控制
烟波上　不明的路
茫然错过　你已闭紧
眼睛

再凄婉的风也叫不住你了
情感的小小棺木
要海做永久坟场

Drift Bottle

an exclamation mark on the sea
waves and wind must stop there
escorted by white flowers

which hand
at what instant
entrusts an important task
to the sea

O heart, drifting on waves
less restrained than a fish
is it an ocean too
an exit sealed by its last will

a chest emptied
one more woe
how does Earth rotate
to create a meeting

who controls the end
on foggy waves   an unknown way
slipped past   and your eyes
shut

even a tragic wind can't call you back
little coffin of sentiments
wants the sea as a cemetery forever

许多许多母亲

像有亿万匹马达在海底发动
海的躯体震荡　　胸脯耸起
洁白的乳浆喷溅
仿佛要把生命的精气喷发殆尽
仿佛整个天地需要它喂养
它挣扎着　　哀吼着
恨不能把心呕出来的样子
使我想起母亲
许多许多母亲
母亲的群体
永远不屈地做着同一件事
当我不得不转过身　　离去
我听见身后的海哭了
整夜整夜地哭
海的哭声被很多人忽略

Many Many Mothers

like millions of motors unleashed undersea
the sea's body shakes   its chest heaving
in a splash of white breast milk
as if spouting the essence of life to its end
as if the universe needed to be fed
it struggles   howls
as if it couldn't wait to vomit its heart
and I think of Mother
many many mothers
a community
relentlessly working on the same chore
when I've no choice but to turn around   and leave
I hear the sea crying behind me
crying all night and all night
many ignore these sea cries

自己的海

海就在旁边
坐在石头上晒太阳的老渔妇
整半天没看海一眼
她的房子在不远处
知道天黑了海还在那里
过年了海还在那里

而我从别处来
坐了很长时间的车
我是要把海看回去的
一整天地看
使劲地看
一寸一寸地往下看
一丈一丈地往远看
有意无意的海
城府很深的海
什么也没被我看见的海

就在我的脑神经旁边
在返城的车的旁边
在书桌旁边
在床的旁边
像一个装着沸水的大锅

有一个属于自己的海真好
去哪里就能带到哪里
——去菜市场　去会议室　去医院

My Own Sea

the sea is close
an old fisherwoman who tans on a rock
does not even glance at it
she lives nearby
and knows the sea is still there after dark
it is still there after New Year's Day

but I come from elsewhere
after a long ride
I want to bring the sea back
look at it all day long
with all my might
look into it inch by inch
look across it foot by foot
sought or unsought
the shrewd sea
I can't see

right by my cranial nerves
by the car back to the city
by my desk
and bed
like a wok of boiling water

how lovely to have your own sea
to bring it with you wherever you go
—to the market   the meeting room   the hospital

在陪伴年迈母亲的日子里
我就把它放在那古旧的藤椅旁边
看着它波涛翻滚

when I keep my old mother company
I put it by an ancient rattan chair
and watch its waves toss

用了两个海

今天我经历了两个海
一个是形而上的——
透彻　湛蓝　打碎又集合起的玻璃一样　夹杂着锋利
不停止地切割　穿刺　折射着金星般的辉芒
海滩明亮圣洁　似乎只允许眼睛和心灵行走
被称作抽象画廊的石壁　每一根线条
要整个天地共破译

另一个是世俗的　有点浑浊　蓝中带着土黄
很多的养殖船　像忙碌的大叔大婶　健康　富足　身无旁顾
饱和的阳光把他们周身涂得暖洋洋
海风使海轻轻摇晃　天庭祥和地罩在头顶　商量了似的
——要照顾好他们
我心里的祝福　没有资格说出来

我知道它们是同一个海
有着同一条海岸线　只拐了一座村庄
在深处没有区别

我的一首诗　一条命
就用了两个海

Using Two Seas

I experience two seas today
one is metaphysical—
transparent azure   like glass shattered and reassembled   a mix of
    sharp edges
cutting non-stop   piercing   refracting rays like Venus
pure bright shore   as if only eyes and soul could walk across
the cliff an abstract art gallery   each line
to be deciphered by heaven and earth

the other is secular   a little murky   yellow-brown in blue
aquaculture vessels   like busy uncles and aunts   healthy   rich   no
    worries no woes
saturated light smears over their warm bodies
breeze sways the sea   a sky above in harmony   as if all were decided
—take good care of them
I can't lay claim   to this blessing in my heart

I know they are one sea
with one coastline   around one village
no difference deep down

a poem of mine   a life
two seas used

海滩上的一只狗

那只狗朝着大海咳叫
小小的头　一突一突的
它把那一排排扑来的浪潮看成什么呢
也朝着扑去

可刚靠近　它们又退下去
使它愣在那　不知如何是好
只好又对着海大叫
呼出一团团新鲜的热气

它的叫声大约能传出几丈远吧
海潮的轰响覆盖而来
它忽然就找不到自己的声音了
可不一会儿
又孤独地暴露出来

于是就一遍遍地试验　像要弄清楚什么
每天都来　叫得后腿都弯下去
有些游客捡起石头朝它扔
也顾不得回应

直到有一天
它跑到附近的山头
眼睛里有了一片退远的海　苍茫无边
才怔怔的蹲下　长久地……

A Dog on the Shore

facing the sea the dog whined
a little head   up and down
what did it see in these rushing rows of tide
it too rushed forward

but once it was near   they backed down
staring blankly   it did not know what to do
but to howl at the sea
puffing out whirls of fresh hot air

its howls could reach many feet out
tides thundered
suddenly the dog couldn't find its voice
but in no time
it reappeared on its own

again and again like an experiment   as if to clarify
it came every day   barking until its hind legs bent
tourists picked up stones to throw at the dog
but it was lost in thought

until one day
it ran to a mountaintop nearby
a sea fading in its eyes   vast and edgeless
it crouched down in a daze   for a long time . . .

没有可以把你盖起来的道具

你是一个道具
用来比照　感知
人们轻松了　通透了　或更沉重茫然
现在　你是一个搅动不停的伤口　一个满是泪光的眼睛
没有可以把你盖起来的道具

当我在城市的墙里
想着你赤裸在远方的黑暗下
我就和你一起不睡　这一刻与下一刻
隔着一个深渊的翻来覆去

No Prop Can Shield You

you are a prop
used for contrast   perception
people relax   free   or in a heavier daze
now   you are a stirring wound   an eye full of tears
no prop can shield you

in the walls of a city
thinking of you naked and far in the dark
I'll stay awake with you   this instant and next
divided by the tossing and turning of an abyss

看夕阳

好大好红的夕阳
可惜被楼房挡住只露出个边角
我跑到书房的窗口
看到它的左边一半
我跑到厨房的窗口
看到它右边的一半
我在屋子里跑来跑去
想那夕阳也是想深情地看我一眼

Look at the Sunset

how large, how red the setting sun
blocked by a building it shows only a rim
I run to the study window
to see its left half
I run to the kitchen window
to see its right half
I run to and fro
thinking the sun also longs to peek at me

红土

被锄头挖去皮的荒山
露出鲜艳的红土
像饱浸着血
像一大片伤口
我童年居住的村庙　祠堂
就在这样的荒山
母亲在里面教山民的孩子读书
记忆中全是大雷雨　蝙蝠　鬼怪的传说
被母亲垦出的红土
残阳里像炭火一样恐怖
和我脆弱的情感连在一起的红土
现在被很疼地址出来
我无法参与人们赞美红土
就像我难以和人们谈论故居

Red Earth

the ruined mountain whose skin is scraped
reveals the fresh red earth
as a huge wound
soaked in blood
I spent my childhood in a village temple   a shrine
in a ruined mountain like this
where Mother taught the mountain children to read
memories are all about storms and bats   legends of ghosts and monsters
at dusk the red earth Mother plowed
looked as scary as a charcoal fire
linked to my fragile emotions
red earth is now ripped in pain
I can never join others in praise of the red earth
just as it is hard for me to discuss my hometown

那野山里

小路　溪湾　田地是过去的
风和阳光也是过去的
而我已不是过去的了
再停留　再回望
也只能把它们留在这野山里

暴雨的时候　酷暑的时候
我会想念它们　想念那个
在上面行走的女孩

但总有一天
再也没有一个人这样凭窗想它们了
那野山里曾有过的一切
会不会因一个人的消失而消失

In That Wild Mountain

small paths   creek bends   and fields were the past
wind and sunlight too
but I am no longer the past
even if I linger   and look back
I can only leave them behind in the wild mountain

in thunderstorms   high summer
I long for them   long for
that girl walking over them

but someday
no one will long for them by the window
would all that belonged to the wild mountain
disappear as one disappears

大雨

大雨　　敲窗
起身收起屋外的衣裳
抬头看远方
父亲坟上的一小块水泥
该被击得好响

父亲是否也在看着大雨
想着世间的苦难
那野道上是否还有生灵
满脸是水

有些东西永收不到屋里来
永在大雨里

Heavy Rain

heavy rain   strikes the window
I get up to remove clothes hung outside
and look afar
the cement patch on Father's tomb
must be struck aloud

is Father also watching this heavy rain
thinking about worldly suffering
are there creatures on the wild path
faces ravaged by water

some things are never kept indoors
they stay forever in the rain

刻在墓石上的名字

我的名字已刻在山里的一块墓石上
我的名字和父亲名字的区别是
父亲的涂着黑漆　我的是红漆

从此就经常想念那两个字
想它们在满山虫鸣中寂静的样子
想那两个做了我名字的字
无遮无栏在风雨里
也想父亲的两个字　为何要用黑的
想妈妈姐姐和妹妹的　和我一样
都还红色地在父亲旁边

每次扫完墓离开前
总要把那些字看了又看
把旁边的树木花草看了又看
把当时在场的一两只昆虫
头顶的天空和云朵也看了看
希望它们好好做朋友

别的墓石上
也密密麻麻地刻着儿孙们的名字
它们的主人此刻都在哪里……

Names on the Tombstone

my name is carved on a mountain tombstone
my name is different from Father's
his is painted black   mine red

I often think of those two characters
their stillness in a mountain of insect cries
the two characters that make up my name
unsheltered in rain and wind
wondering why the two characters in Father's name   must be in black
why Mother's and my sisters'   like mine
are red by his side

before I leave   after cleaning the tomb
I always look at those characters
their surrounding trees and flowers
one or two insects there
the sky and clouds
hoping they are friends

densely carved on other tombstones
the names of children and grandchildren
where are their owners now . . .

这单独来的风

这么说有一缕风在橱子旁边
把那张画纸翻过去　又翻过去
有一缕风一直没走

别的东西都没动
这么说这一缕风纤细的
只能掀动那张画纸

没有一个人的客厅
一张画纸忽然翻过去
怎么不觉得奇怪
怎么不算是事件

这单独来的风
经过哪些山脊
怎样进了我的客厅
如果没有那张翻动的画纸
我还不知道呢

This Wind Comes Alone

so it goes, a wind by an armoire
turns the drawing paper   over and over
a wind that never goes away

other things stay still
so it goes, this fine wind
stirring just a drawing paper

no one in the living room
a drawing paper suddenly turns
why isn't this strange
why isn't it an event

this wind comes alone
across what ridge
how did it enter my living room
if not for the paper tossing and turning
I'd not know

一块阳光

风把窗帘动一下
阳光就像金块一样闪了一下
风又把窗帘动一下
阳光又像金条般晃了一下
只有在昏暗的屋里
阳光才变得像黄金

风在更努力地掀着窗帘
想把那合缝弄大一点
阳光若再大一点就不像黄金了

一墙之外便是满世界的阳光
满世界的金光中间
一个空出的昏暗有多么难
我的手朝那块阳光伸过去
它就伏在我的手背上
暖烘烘的
像另一只手

A Patch of Sunlight

wind tugs the curtain
like a gold nugget sunlight glows
wind tugs again
like a gold bar sunlight swings
only in a dim room
can sunlight turn gold

wind pulls the curtain harder
hoping to widen the seam
sunlight won't be golden once widened

beyond a wall lies a world full of sunlight
amid a world full of golden light
how tough it is for a dim space
I reach for the patch of sunlight
it leans on the back of my hand
warmly
like another hand

一个苍生

一个人飞奔而来
头发和风的方向对抗
那是昨晚枕上辗转的塑造
呼啦啦拨开围着小店的民工
抓住电话筒就像抓住性命
听不见他在嘶喊什么
沸腾的噪音似高厚的静寂
一些新鲜的血丝倏忽灭去
钻出人堆时
眼睛里已有云雾弥漫
飘飘忽在人流车流中避闪了几次
一个骤然停顿脑壳里有什么被扳倒了
他脚步松懈下来　伸了伸臂
看见阳光满天满地
可是路边又有一个电话蹲着似魂灵
他的皮夹克鼓胀起来
终于像老鹰一样扑过去

A Common Life

a man races by
his hair against the wind
shaped by the toss and turns on a pillow last night
shoving past peasant workers in a shop
grabbing the telephone like grabbing a life
you can't hear what he's yelling
bubbles of noise like a tall thick stillness
fresh strands of blood suddenly gone
emerging from the crowd
his eyes are shrouded with clouds and fog
wandering and dodging among men and cars
as if something stops and topples in his brain
he slows down his footsteps   stretches his arms
sees sunlight everywhere
yet another phone squats by the road like a spirit
his leather jacket bloats up
and he pounces on it like an eagle

在一座枫林旁边

秋天的富翁们都在这儿啊
这些谢顶的长者
满地的黄叶似撕碎的残稿
现在只需用银灰色的枝条
就能搂抱住高空的殿宇

那些骨节里走走停停的力量
一定像珠珠粒粒的蒸馏水
先一点一点穿透自己
似那种层层镂空的象牙柱
哪一层转动都会变化出不同的窗口　眼睛

它们站在那里
意趣交汇出一个逼人的空间
使我不得不一次次退出　体会自己的阻塞

它们不再给你碎碎的风　小勺子般的爱和抚慰
它们已经使头顶的雁　变得很轻

它们的枝条漫不经心地摇摆着
是有灵魂出去散步　还是骨头在做早操
它们每天都在聊些什么呀
它们的话语
怎么像风的声音——
穿过无数回廊的风的声音

By the Maple Woods

here are the millionaires of autumn
balding elders
yellow leaves scattered like torn pieces of manuscript
only silver gray branches
can hold the sky palace

strength must be strolling in those joints
like pearls of distilled water
piercing through   drop by drop
like layers of hollow carved ivory pillars
windows   and eyes mutate at any turn

standing there
their charms conjure a compelling space
forcing me to exit each time   to experience my own barrage

they no longer offer you crisp wind   spoonfuls of love and solace
they've turned the geese above their heads   into lightness

their branches sway casually
is the soul out for a walk   are their bones up for morning exercise
what do they chat about every day
their voices
why do they sound like the wind—
the voice of wind through myriad cloisters

III

两个瓷瓶

第一天　我看见它——
春风　春水　荷花　荷叶　莲蓬
摇摆　迷人　纷乱……
瓶口至底有一尺多深的暗和静
我把手伸进去
像伸进一个凉凉的潭
我抱住它
一直抱到旅馆的房间里

第二天　它在等我——
野山　野树　野溪　野云　石桥　瓦屋
一排淡淡的鸟不知要飞去哪里……
我也去抱住它
像抱着一个故乡
一腔的空
很轻

我把它们抱到回程的火车上　抱到我家客厅
有时它们会一高一低地浮动进烟尘　那年
上海的街头
有很多孤独的瓷瓶

Two Porcelain Vases

the first day   I see it—
spring wind   spring water   lotus   lotus leaf   lotus seed pod
swaying   alluring   swirling . . .
inches of dark and quiet in the vase
I reach my hand inside
like reaching into a cool deep pond
I hug it
all the way to my hotel room

the next day   it waits for me—
wild mountain   wild tree   wild creek   wild cloud   stone bridge
     tiled house
who knows where a misty row of birds might fly . . .
I hug it tight
like hugging a homeland
a chestful of space
very light

I hug them to my return train   to my living room
sometimes they float high and low into dust   this year
in the streets of Shanghai
there are many lonely porcelain vases

一棵老的树

银色的树干　疏朗地张开
没有很细的枝　没有叶子
风暴走得干干净净

被丛林的茂密和阴暗
衬得
如白白的水流
仿佛它植根的山
是一座湖

像不谙世事的老奶奶
连眼泪都是淡的
手指也很凉

回望　只有它
如玉雕
养在天穹的身体里

只有它
像一个烂漫的玩具
吊挂着星斗和天籁
摇起来会叮叮咚咚响
想飞就飞起来

An Old Tree

silver trunk   opens cheerfully
without fine branches   without leaves
the storm has left cleanly

contrasted
by the dense and bleak forest
like white water
as if the mountain where it is rooted
were a lake

like an ignorant old grandmother
even tears are so plain
fingers cold

looking back   only it
like jade sculpture
grows inside heaven's vault

only it
like a carefree toy
droops with stars and sounds of nature
rings like a ding-dong bell when it shakes
flies when it wants to fly away

父亲当年修钟

父亲说
他的钟又会走了
父亲的脸上有奇异的光
父亲是用了什么办法
坚决不让那只小钟死去的

疲惫的父亲
从茶山的小路
回到他的小屋时
有一只活的钟陪着是不一样的

父亲当年修钟
一定比为病人做手术的大夫还揪着心
毕竟在那沉寂的茶山中
只有那只钟
像他身边的一个生命

In Those Days Father Repaired the Clock

Father said
his clock could walk again
Father's face had a strange light
what did he do
not to let the little clock die

when weary Father
returned to his hut
by a path in the tea mountain
things felt different with a clock alive

in those days Father repaired the clock
he must have been more anxious than a surgeon
after all in that silent tea mountain
only that clock
was like a life by his side

新世纪第一天的太阳

回老家的母亲仍把心爱的羽绒被留下
她想留下一点记忆
母亲脆弱的心思
表明人世的悲哀是多么强大

临行时嘱咐要常拿去翻晒
我偶尔记起又懒得动手
直到二零零一年一月一日
新世纪第一天的太阳
在整个天地间向我大喊了一声
我顿时记起母亲的羽绒被
任何活都得先放下
我执行了这个命令

使我疑惑的是
母亲和太阳之间
有着怎样不同寻常的联系
而我随之升起的感动
或许已经进入某种巨大的网络
使我想对全世界的母亲说
妈妈　您的孩子
已经帮您晒了被子

这时
一只不知隐匿在哪里的鸟儿畅快地笑着
一下子推开了朝着天堂的窗户
而我母亲的羽绒被也像一大块黄金似的

Sun on the First Day of the New Century

Mother returned home but left behind her favorite comforter
she wanted to leave some memories behind
Mother's fragile idea
spoke of the strength of worldly sorrow

prior to leaving she told me to sun the comforter regularly
now and then I remembered but was lazy
until January 1, 2001
the sun on the first day of the new century
shouted at me from heaven and earth
right away I recalled Mother's comforter
dropped everything
and carried out her order

what baffled me
was the unusual ties
between a mother and the sun
emotions surging in me
might have entered a gigantic network
urging me to tell mothers worldwide
Mother   your child
has sunned the comforter for you

all at once
a bird hidden nowhere laughed heartily
pushed open the window to heaven
like a chunk of gold Mother's comforter enriched

使这光明的殿宇空前的富有
我感到生命的遗憾不是死亡
而是没有把一个人做足

the glorious palace more than ever
regrets in life struck me not as death
but a life unfulfilled

有没有这样的一只鹰

一

有没有一只鹰在寻找一片花地
看见一只蝴蝶　生起羡慕之心
有没有一只鹰想蹲下来
同情一只在草棚里下蛋的母鸡
有没有一只鹰敢蔑视仰望
不要趁着下雨的时候流泪

有没有一只鹰肯承认　那樱桃大的心脏里
并没有闪电　风暴和冰雹
只有一腔温热的血

二

有没有一只　会心酸的鹰
为生病的小鹰忧愁的鹰　神经衰弱的鹰
说很累的鹰
为什么人们都把鹰说成雄鹰呢

看见云朵了吗
它是多么柔软

Is There Such an Eagle

1

is there an eagle who seeks a flowerbed
sees a butterfly   grows envious
is there an eagle who wants to squat down
pities a hen laying eggs in a hayloft
is there an eagle who dares to scorn reverence
does not cry when it rains

is there an eagle who admits   in its cherry-sized heart
there is no lightning   no storm no hail
just a chestful of warm blood

2

is there an eagle   with a grieved heart
who worries for its sick baby   suffers a nervous breakdown
says *I'm very tired*
why do people always say an eagle is a male

do you see the cloud
it is so tender

无底无边的天空
也像爱　像悲伤
没有方向和结果

畅通不是更密的栅栏吗
没有阻挡不是更不饶人的围困吗
有没有一只鹰因此而谨慎　不安

三

有没有一只鹰肯让意志弯一弯
像被风吹动　让春燕过去的柳丝
或像攀缘大树的藤萝
如果真有这样的大树呢

有没有一只鹰把眼睛放在天外
看见自己渺小的翅膀
说怕　恐惧

有没有一只鹰羽毛纷乱
躺在山冈　对一株小草说：
已竭尽全力
但无法飞完天空

a sky without limits
like love   like sorrow
without direction or consequence

isn't *open* and *clear* a finer barrier
isn't *obstacle free* a harsher siege
is there an eagle who turns guarded   and ill at ease

3

is there an eagle willing to bend its will
like a willow moved by wind   making way for spring swallows
or like a wisteria winding up a tree
if there is such a tree

is there an eagle who sees beyond the sky
sees its own tiny wings
says *I'm scared   I'm terrified*

is there an eagle with feathers in disarray
lies on a hill   tells a strand of grass
all my strength is exhausted
I can't fly the whole sky

春临

感到它有大山一样的体积
隆重　苍翠　就在身旁
马路涨挤了
迎面而来的人惊异我满面春风

和大山一样的春天一起走
会以为自己是一座小山
直到撞上十字路口
才羞愧地看了看车水马龙的四周

才知道轰隆隆的春天
并不只为一人移动
我体内的溪水
连着多么壮阔的洪流

Spring Arrives

it feels like the volume of a mountain
grand   green   right by my side
the road is packed
everyone is taken by my beaming face

I walk with the mountain-like spring
thinking I am a hill
until I run into a crossroad
looking abashed at the traffic flow

realizing the thundering spring
does not move for just a man
the stream in my body
links to so majestic a torrent

一只鸟儿

一只鸟儿
落在一堆废铁上
从一块铁板跳到另一块铁板
又弹向　翘起的细铁条的顶端
像一个音符
对付很大的乐器

一些锈屑落下　又一些落下
它和废铁们　仿佛为这
要笑出声来

好心情的鸟儿
这时看见了我的眼睛
叫了两声　却不指望回答

鸟儿其实已经动了我的心
惊动了整个阴沉的下午

A Bird

a bird
lands on a pile of scrap iron
jumps from one iron plank to another
then bounces   to the tip of a thin tilting rod
like a note
handling a very large musical instrument

rust falls   and more
the bird and the scrap iron   seem
to laugh aloud

the cheerful bird
sees my eyes now
chirps twice   but asks for no reply

the bird has actually moved my heart
astonishing the whole gloomy afternoon

一株菜花

一株菜花在阴影边缘
它的五个花杯盛着满满的阳光
三只蝴蝶在畅饮
风想把倾斜的花枝扶正
它摇晃的样子很天真

有一只醉了的蝴蝶吊在一片瓣上
使那朵花深深弯下
花朵多么柔弱
娇嫩的花瓣却没有破碎

风和太阳瞬息变化
花儿的敏感令我心疼

有一串蕾等待开放
像千手佛没张开掌心
只有一根细茎的菜花
把一个很大的春天放在身上

A Bouquet of Cauliflower

a bouquet of caulifower at the edge of a silhouette
five flower cups beaming with sunlight
three butterflies are drinking heartily
wind wants to straighten a slanted stem
it looks innocent when it sways

a drunk butterfly hangs on a petal
the flower stoops down lowly
so tender and weak
but soft petals aren't broken

wind and sun metamorphose in an instant
my heart aches from the flowers' sensitivity

a string of buds awaits the bloom
like a thousand Buddha hands with palms closed
only a cauliflower with a thin stem
places a huge spring on its body

金盏菊

这融进旭日的最小之湖
这停歇光芒的最小厅堂
被怎样的决心打开
连接春天万千路径
无数蜜黄的流程
怎样紊乱

悲伤已被蜜蜂吮走
金杯难盛痴情万片
蝴蝶腹下小小火山
能表达的只有焚毁

无言已把话说尽
金盏菊
金盏菊
浅浅的深渊

Marigold

this smallest lake merges with the rising sun
this smallest hall stops rays of light
what perseverance can open them
linking thousands of spring roads
a myriad flow of honey-yellow
how chaotic

bees have sucked away sorrow
golden cups can't hold blind passion
little volcanoes under butterfly bellies
burning is their only expression

silence has said it all
marigold
marigold
shallow abyss shallow

康乃馨

谁注意过康乃馨花瓣边缘的锯齿
谁知道这温馨名字掩盖的血性

一朵花从什么时候开始磨炼利器
一朵花怎样在生命里设了栅栏
　　说过一千次不要

美在悬崖的中途
香是渊底磐石
渴望碰弯一次强风

全身的血紧握在一个拳中
举在命定的结局之上
不让我的思路通过
不让危险的眼睛看穿

Carnation

who notices the teeth of a saw on the edge of a carnation petal
who knows the courage masked by this warm fragrant name

when does a flower begin forging its weapon
how does a flower build fences in life
    saying no a thousand times

beauty is midway up a cliff
fragrance is a rock in deep waters
longing to bend a strong wind

blood from the whole body is clenched in a fist
above the destined end
preventing my line of thought to pass through
and dangerous eyes to see through

孕妇

春天袍襟的深处
孕妇　如大花
缓慢着色
风在每一片瓣沿守卫
要蝴蝶离开

满天空的云堆叠在眼帘
整个田野谈论她睡眠的理由
煦阳把河水热了一遍又一遍
暖活一湖涟漪
一个指针在零点的小钟要开始走动

谁问过孕妇愿不愿意
谁知道她的每一片肌肤
都是防御的盾
在闹嚷嚷的春天中央
就要被打开最后一道门

这是胜利还是惨败
春天贪婪把万物引诱
风变肥　雾变瘦
花到了非开不可的时候
春天和孕妇之间
还有什么可以理清

The Pregnant Woman

deep inside the robe of spring
the pregnant woman   like a big flower
in gradual shades
wind guards each petal
wants the butterfly to leave

clouds in piles
the fields discuss her sleep
over and over the sun warms up the river
warming alive a lake to its ripples
at midnight the clock hand starts to move

who has asked if the woman is willing
who knows that her skin is each piece
a defense shield
at the heart of a boisterous spring
the last door about to open

is this a victory or sheer defeat
spring greedily lures all creatures
wind fattens   fog thinning
it is time to flower
between spring and this pregnant woman
what else to clear

水啊……

当时和我在一起的
还有一棵树　两只白鸟
水就在旁边说话
这一片水是那一片水的耳朵
它们互相听着
有时候很多水在问一片水
那一片水就抽出一串漩涡来
　　　解开　再解开……

世界是没有方向的
所以到处都是方向
水迷路　流浪
茫然又一心一意
到了一个水的广场
许多许多的水在隆重徘徊
许多许多的水的长袍拖来拖去
一个怎样的举动已酝酿千年

有推动巨石的声音
那是水在推动自己的心脏

水把心脏推到悬崖上撕开
一缕一缕地
洗涤　看清　再烧透

O Water . . .

along with me
a tree   two white birds
water is chatting by the side
a piece of water is another's ear
listening to each other
sometimes many waters ask a piece of water
that pulls out a string of whirlpools
    loosening   and again . . .

the world has no direction
everywhere is a direction
water loses its way   and wanders
lost yet firm
arriving at a water square
where many waters loiter in grandeur
and drag their long gowns
what's brewing these last thousand years

the sound of pushing a megalith
is water pushing its own heart

water pushes its heart to a cliff and tears it apart
strand by strand
washed   seen   and burned

熊熊的水
　　熄灭下来
　　　熄灭下来
　　　　熄灭下来
水的烟雾是很小很轻的一粒粒水

blazing water
   fades out
     fades out
      fades out
water smoke—very tiny very light water grains

鸟鸣春日

鸟鸣在跳着
一粒一粒弹下峻岭
　　　　跃上岩石
　　　　落下溪潭
挑拨起一块一块的寂静

鸟鸣在跳着
一队队在这座山头
一列列在那座山头
攀着初雾的肩膀
利索地在空中接起来

鸟鸣在山腰做着游戏
拉扯着云彩
要阳光绕开一点
　　　破开一点
　　　变一点花样
　　　不要那么整齐

鸟鸣给有点散漫有点迟钝的春天引路
　　一架阶梯一样降下
　　　　一架阶梯一样降下
　　　　　　一架阶梯一样降下

Bird Call on a Spring Day

bird calls leap
grain by grain bounce off a cliff
      up the rocks
      down a stream
rustling silence piece by piece

bird calls leap
team by team on this mountaintop
row by row on that mountaintop
climb the shoulder of early fog
connect swiftly in mid-sky

bird calls play on the mountainside
tug at clouds
widen the coil of light
    crack it
    transfigure it
    avoid neatness

bird calls guide the way for the lazy slow spring
    like a flight of stairs they fall
      like a flight of stairs they fall
        like a flight of stairs they fall

快乐

雨丝西斜
我知道南边有一些风
到处都是淅沥的声响
我知道到处都有扬起的面庞
花叶抖动　藤蔓飘摇
我知道大地此刻有无数的快乐
因为一阵春雨　一袭南风
来自我们目力无法到达的地方

Joy

rain is slanting west
I know a wind from the south
sprinkling sounds everywhere
I know uplifted faces everywhere
flowers and leaves quiver   vines sway
I know the earth has countless joys now
because a spring rain   a southern wind
come from somewhere our eyes can't reach

它们还是没出来

那玉兰丛里藏着什么呢
一只喜鹊飞进去长久不出来
一只麻雀夹了一下翅膀进去也不出来
一只蝴蝶出来逗了一圈
又飞进去
再也没见出来

风使叶片动了
荫影的长廊该会摇摇晃晃
它们还是没有出来

They Still Have Not Emerged

what hides in the magnolia bush
a magpie flew in and did not come out after a long time
a sparrow flapped its wings and flew in, but did not come out
a butterfly emerged and flirted around
flew back in
but has not been out since

wind moves the leaves
the long hall of shadows must be swaying
they still have not emerged

水流的声音

水流的声音格尔格尔的
水流的声音是——
　　　　透明叠着透明的
一溪的鹅卵石一凸一凸的脊背
一溪的鹅卵石一凹一凹的腹部

一溪的透明的脊背　　透明的腹部
　　　　抚摩过来
格尔格尔地从我身上滑过
我的身体是不是
一溪的鹅卵石

Voice of Flowing Water

the voice of flowing water is giggling
the voice of flowing water is—
    transparency layered with transparency
a stream of pebbles with protruding backs
a stream of pebbles with intruding bellies

a stream of transparent backs   transparent bellies
    caressing
gliding over my body in giggles
is my body
a stream of pebbles

在原野上

第一缕风是从那小山后来的
它先推开我胸口的一小片窗
接着　更多的风就从桉树林　菜花地
一齐扑来
我密封好好的身体　难以闭拢
云朵和蝴蝶直接进去

经络的衔接处
有了蜜滴和露水
血脉的细小巷道
阳光的手来去

把一些东西赶到远的地方被更大的风吹走
让大脑变成快乐的鸟巢
心脏如嗡嗡响的花团

In the Open Field

behind the hill comes the first wind
pushing open a small window in my chest
then   more winds from the jarrah trees   the rapeflower field
all in a rush
my well-sealed body   can hardly stay shut
clouds and butterflies are diving in

the juncture of meridians
now honey and dew
in the alleys of blood flow
sunlight like a hand comes to and fro

let's drive some things far away to a stronger wind
let the brain turn into a happy nest
the heart a team of humming flowers

IV

永恒

永恒不是直线的
它像蒲公英炸开的花　心脏的放射性疼痛
无数方向地飞出去　刺出去
宇宙在我们不知道的时候
爆炸了一遍又一遍

永恒不是没有尽头　而是没有边缘
自己把自己弄得没有外面
没有一枚针
替它刺一个洞

因为那针
也在帮着建构永恒

一被当成永恒　就没办法了

Eternal

eternity isn't a straight line
like an exploding dandelion   pain radiating from a heart
it flies in countless directions   it shoots out
when we are unaware   the universe
explodes again and again

eternity isn't endless   but marginless
it ends up having no exterior
not one needle
can pierce a hole in it

because the needle
also helps build eternity

once viewed as eternal   it is over

据说

鱼的眼睛总是圆睁着
活着时被风暴冲击咸水浸泡也睁着
死时只剩下一根脊柱一个头　也睁着
有的还睁得眼珠都掉出来
表明它是最新鲜的　活蹦乱跳着去蒸的
表明烧它的火是多么旺

据说鱼没有眼帘　无论如何
也不能闭起眼睛

鱼的骨头是刺
在内部刺穿自己
鳍像钢针
在外部刺着海
为了能游起来
还要摆动

据说鱼没有泪腺
永远流不出眼泪
据说海
全是泪水

They Say

fish eyes always stare wide open
even when alive   struck by storms or soaked in salt water
or dead with just a spine a head
some stare so hard their eyeballs drop
fish is indeed freshest   it flops when steamed
fire for cooking fish is indeed blazing

they say fish have no eyelids   no matter what
their eyes can't shut

fish bones are thorns
piercing fish from the inside
fins like steel needles
piercing sea on the outside
in order to swim
they even vibrate

they say fish have no tear glands
fish never shed tears
they say the sea
is all tears

风来了 风走了

风来了
像许多手
把满桌的书页
翻得哗哗响 我看见
91年书刊的封面 又看见
92年的 93年的 我忘记了
它们已堆在这里这么多年
它们沉默不响
它们有没有喊过
世界啊
我在这

那些钉在纸页上的文字
如果没有人去读它就死了
一本合起的书
像寝床
也像棺木

但风来了
那样认真地
翻动着
有时停止片刻
像在思索 接着又
更加细心地翻找
那些写书的人
曾经也这样
翻着纸页

Wind Comes Wind Goes

wind comes
like many hands
shuffling through pages on the table
noisily   I see
magazine covers of '91   and
those from '92   '93   I've forgotten
they've been piled up here for so many years
not a word
did they ever yell
O world
I'm here

words pinned on paper
will die if unread
a closed-up book
like a bed
a coffin

but wind comes
so seriously
shuffling
sometimes it stops for a second
as if pondering   then
it peers around more carefully
those who write books
once shuffled
papers like this

风就这样

把已故的时间

翻来翻去

我看着白花花的书桌

很象一座荒草凄迷的孤岛

有一张书页

竟然脱离了书脊

满屋飞飘

落在地上

又跃起来

我看它仅差一点就够着窗户了

就这一刻

风走了

wind too
shuffling dead time
here and there
I look at the messy-white desk
like an island of weeds

a page
abandons the book spine
drifts around the room
falls on the ground
then leaps again
see, it's so close to reaching the window
just right then
wind is gone

一挂飘忽的楼梯

别人以为你睡了
可你脑子里的河山正在展开
高山　大海都能调遣来
天庭湛蓝完整　白云飘
繁忙的街道从中穿过
一个模糊的聚会　在年代的远景里

后来你真的睡着了
就仿佛进入天堂或地狱
这里走走　那里瞧瞧　推门进去
已故的亲人都神采奕奕

猛然睁开眼睛
又是一个世界　很亮　有声有色
似乎还有一个地下室
自动封闭起来

如果把一个人简化再简化
就是一挂飘忽的楼梯
在尘世的各处碰来撞去

A Flight of Floating Stairs

others think you are asleep
landscapes unfolding in your mind
high mountains   oceans can be assigned here
a full and azure sky   white clouds float
a bustling street weaves through
a hazy reunion   of a past era

later you indeed fall asleep
as if in heaven or hell
wandering here   looking there   pushing open a door
dead kin are all glowing with health

eyes suddenly open
yet another world   very bright   very vivid
and a basement perhaps
sealing up by itself

if you simplify a man again and again
he will just become a flight of floating stairs
knocking here and there in this world of dust

雨越下越大

雨溅在屋顶
像溅在脑壳

溅　就是拒绝
就是有硬的一面

火封闭自己成烟
红玛瑙的血丝冰凉
大海也不能上岸

天空怎么就没有
可以关起自己的门

雨越下越大
终于进到心里

终于和雨抱成团
汹涌成雨

Rain Pours Harder

rain splashes on the roof
as if on a skull

splash   is refusal
with a hard face

fire sealed as smoke
icy strands of carnelian blood
even the sea can't move ashore

why can't the sky
have a door that shuts itself

rain pours harder
at last into my heart

at last I join the rain
soaring as rain

昨天的雨和今天的雨连起来

昨天在黄昏的路上
暴雨突临
挤进廊桥下黑黑的人堆里
听雨在每个身体里黑黑地越下越沉

今天
仍阴着
终又下起了雨
昨天的雨和今天的雨就连起来

不同的是我在家里
感觉它在对屋顶发脾气　却是冲着我的

我的骨头空空
吸着白晃晃的凉气
不知何时
屋顶上的雨已归去

Yesterday's Rain Joins Today's Rain

yesterday on the dusky road
a storm suddenly struck
I squeezed myself into the black mass of people under a bridge
listening to rain sink into blackness in each body

today
the sky is still dark
at last rain pours again
yesterday's rain joins today's rain

this time I am at home
feeling its tantrum at the rooftop   its tantrum at me

my empty bones
breathe the white cool air
not knowing when
rain on the rooftop has already left

以剪的形式

鸟儿叫　一窝窝剪刀似的
剪啊剪
在空气里　在树丛中
生机勃勃　辉芒四射

鸟儿也在我的心尖
剪了一下　又剪了一下
一再地以剪的形式
提醒我

鸟儿不知道
人的心是不能剪的

In the Form of a Scissor Cut

bird calls   like nests of scissors
cut and cut
in air   in trees
vibrant   radiant

birds too are at the tip of my heart
cut here   cut there
over and over in the form of a scissor cut
reminding me

birds don't know
you can't cut hearts

我们闻到的浓香

玉兰花刚出蕾时像冒头的剑
香从根里爬上主干通向枝茎
到达那剑柄之下　每进去一点　剑就伸长一点
直到被挤得裂开　变成一瓣瓣小小的刀
我们闻到的浓香　似乎有
一缕一缕的形状

The Aroma We Smell

a magnolia bud sprouts up like the tip of a sword
its fragrance climbs from root to stem and branches
arriving beneath the hilt   it enters a little   the sword lengthens a little
till it cracks open   into petals of small knives
the aroma we smell   seems to have
the shape of a plume

鸟儿已经飞走了

鸟儿又在我周围叫　一叫
我的神志就被叫了去
就停止了手头正在做的事情

鸟儿叫——
一簇簇正在开的花似的
一串串涌动的水泡似的
我的心就成了花树　成了湖
半天也安静不下来

可鸟儿已经飞走了
鸟儿一飞走就像是永别

Birds Have Already Flown Away

birds are calling around me again   a call
my mind is called away
so I stop what I'm doing

birds call—
like clusters of blooming flowers
like strings of billowy bubbles
my heart turns into a flower tree   a lake
for a long while it can't calm down

but birds have already flown away
when birds fly away it seems like goodbye

想起你的出生

当我的身体
棉纸般薄在产床上
护士正把你昂起的粘着血点的四肢
摁到盛着水的盆里

是此刻黄昏虚弱的红日
使我想起你的出生

看见一个更大的盛水的盆
等着接纳它

Recalling Your Birth

when my body
lay thin on a delivery bed   like cotton paper
the nurse pressed your dangling bloodstained limbs
into a basin of water

this dusky frail red sun
recalls your birth to me

as I see a larger basin of water
waiting to receive it

平安地带

绿灯
斑马线
脚步是朝前的
心却提防着别的方向
心哦　总是做着最艰难的事情

那么多迎面而来的心
摇摇拽拽

Safety Zone

green light
zebra crossing
footsteps race forward
yet the heart is wary of other directions
O heart   always tackling the toughest task

so many hearts onrushing
swaying, tugging

九曲溪

仙人的隐喻
被解说淡化
深幽的心绪模糊

谁安排这一刻
九曲穿行
水呵
都是同样面容
怎能把真情辨认

无数透明的脚奔跑
会在哪个水潭停留
又把深渊的心
放在一盏芳杯中
幸福地枯干

忘却　会圆满情感的事迹
青山　不能老站在往事中

Creek of Nine Tunes

a fairy metaphor
explained and diluted
blurring moods deep down

who arranges this instant
nine tunes interweave
O waters
all of a same face
how can we recognize sincerity

transparent legs run
which pool will they stop by
put the abyss' heart
into a fragrant cup
to wither in bliss

oblivion   fulfills the event of sentiments
green mountain   can't stand in bygones forever

金蝴蝶

花儿与花儿之间
振颤的薄翅
如锋利的刀片
要切割去什么
满眼是忧虑的弧线
一千只蝴蝶
把我分散

跟随蝴蝶去历险
我不知道
蝴蝶的道路

彩羽是绝壁的碎片
风砌的阶梯
庞大的春天动荡

猜不透一只忽然停住的蝴蝶
是等待　还是准备放弃
整个天空
围着这一小块金色的悲郁

Golden Butterfly

between flower and flower
thin wings quiver
like sharp razor blades
slicing off something
eyes filled with arcs of anxiety
a thousand butterflies
disperse me

in an adventure with butterflies
I don't know
the way of butterflies

colored plumes are fragments of a cliff
ladders formed by wind
a majestic spring riot

I can't tell if a butterfly suddenly stops
to wait   or give up
the whole sky
surrounds this golden piece of sorrow

瞬间

一只啄米的鸡
它的宁静固定了氤氲气流
像闭锁的湖
黄昏也无法进入

而我知道
这个精巧的机器
可以由一把小刀拆开
再也无法组装

残留的米粒
联系着一个逝去的瞬间
被更多的瞬间淹没

In an Instant

a hen pecks at rice
its calm fixes the flow of mist
like a locked lake
even dusk can't enter

but I know
this delicate machine
can be opened by a knife
and never reassembled back

a last grain of rice
links to a lost instant
flooded by even more instants

童话

大海里的鱼多么自如
丛林中的鸟儿多么欢快
大海和丛林
是没有墙的家

城市有很多的房子
所有的房子都有门牌和锁

心是会疼的地方
过道和小窗都是带血的裂口
大灰狼和喜鹊都远远绕开它

天空是最大的屋子
只有风和空气能住到永久

Fairy Tale

fish in the sea are so free
birds in the woods, so joyful
sea and woods
are houses with no walls

there are many houses in the city
all of them have door plaques and locks

heart is a place that can ache
aisles and windows are cracks with blood
gray wolves and magpies bypass them from afar

the sky is the biggest house
only wind and air can live and last in it

孤独

我看见很大的孤独
像一个巨人　在路的那头
眼前的孤独如一个幼小的孩子
朝它迈动

Solitude

I see a huge solitude
like a giant   at the end of the road
the solitude with me now is like a little child
wheeling toward it

因为有醒

平坦着　几小时
脑子空着

不知何时
空也没了

因为有醒
才知那是睡着了

以前失眠是
一小库的兵器
搏斗在无边的黑暗里

空是生命艰难周密培育馈赠的果子

一个又一个
连接着……

Because of Awakening

plainly   for a few hours
the brain is empty

since when
even emptiness is gone

because of awakening
I know sleep

insomnia was once
a small cache of weapons
wrestling in the edgeless dark

emptiness a fruit a gift that life breeds arduously and finely

one after another
bridging together . . .

沙雕

海一再地控制自己的舌头
直到风暴翻卷而来

海说
我没办法的
还好皇宫里的皇帝也是沙做的
再进去一点就是真的村庄了

风暴说
我也没办法的
背后是什么
逼迫着

Sand Sculpture

sea controls its tongue again
until the storm whirls

sea says
I have no choice
thank God the emperor in the palace is too made of sand
a real village exists further inside

storm says
I too have no choice
what is behind
is driving on

火山石

黑灰
密穿着孔洞　很轻
第一次感到石头也有躯壳
当火焰被抽拔而去

我捡了一块
放在案头
看着会想起大山
和它内部的积抑

想那些从冰峰里冒出的熔岩
如何在白皑皑的天地里哧哧地烙

想海底的火山
即使爆发　仍受整座海的重压
使焚烧的疼痛格外长久

摸一摸
即使是躯壳
也那么硬　麻剌剌的

Volcanic Stone

black gray
densely pierced with holes   very light
for the first time I feel the body of a stone
with flames pulled away

I pick one up
put it on the desk
seeing it I think of the mountain
and its suppressed interior

think of lava pouring from the icy peak
how it irons out in an expanse of white

think of the submarine volcano
even if it erupts   it will still suffer the ocean weight
its pain in flames will last especially long

touch it
even if it is a body
it still feels so hard   like pins and spikes

鹰的黑影涂暗了风暴

那时　我的眼睛
在祠堂的窗洞里
鹰来了　在那么高的地方
把威慑的力量传下来

母鸡的翅膀木板门般打开
小鸡们从各处滚了进去
一只跑得最远的
被鹰的爪子拎了起来

后来　我在一座小庙里读书
庙外的旷野就是课间活动的场所
鹰也常来　在天顶一圈一圈地盘旋
俯视着仰望的孩子

如今　我居住的地方
已经没有鹰了
但有人在好几重山后看见它

鹰去的地方
总是有恐惧的心灵和蛮荒的事物
所有的现代文明都无法灌输到鹰的意识里
所有的科技革命都不能改变鹰

在世界不宁的背景里
鹰的黑影涂暗了风暴

The Eagle's Shadow Darkens the Storm

at that time   my eyes
were in the window opening of a memorial hall
the eagle came   at such a height
spreading the force of deterrence

the hen's wings opened like wooden doors
little chickens tumbled in from all corners
one ran the farthest
lifted up by the eagle's claws

later   I studied in a little shrine
the wilderness outside was the site for school activities
the eagle often came   spiraled in the sky
looked down at children who gazed up high

now   where I live
there is no eagle
but someone has seen it beyond the mountains

places where the eagle goes
always breed fear and savage things
modern civilization can't be instilled into the eagle's consciousness
scientific revolution can't evolve the eagle

in the troubled backdrop of the world
the eagle's shadow darkens the storm

老是一个月亮关在里面

老是白亮亮的天井
老是空洞洞的巷道
老是一片黑屋顶冒烟
老是一道涧水发出响声
老是准时到达脚背的阳光
老是一只狗忽然叫起来
老是歇满乌鸦的乌桕树
老是一只牛犁田　　两只羊吃草
几只母鸡咕咕叫
老是没有一个人上来的岭头
老是一个女孩坐在门槛上
老是那几座山冈　　几片云　　几颗星星
老是一个边缘不变的天
老是一个月亮关在里面

Always a Moon Locked Inside

always a white and bright patio
always an empty lane
always a gush of smoke from the black roof
always the sound of a mountain stream
always the sunlight reaching an instep on time
always a dog that suddenly barks
always a chicken tree full of resting crows
always an ox plowing the field   two goats eating grass
a few hens clucking
always a summit no one has reached
always a girl sitting on the doorsill
always those knolls   some clouds   few stars
always a sky with an unchanging fringe
always a moon locked inside

再说湖

水被围起来就成了湖
人们不在意它从哪里来　怎么来
和那不断汇入　相应流走　以及湖底的涌泉
不在意它的回流冲撞　缠绕纠结
如重叠的密纹唱片
可以抽扯出柔肠百转　往事今生

世上有很多湖
有的已结冰　有的滚烫在火山之巅
有的比海水咸涩
大多数都清凉凉绿汪汪的赏心悦目

沉静是自己压着自己
不知不觉镇住许多东西

Lake, Again

water becomes lake when bounded
people don't care where it comes from   how it comes about
nor about the converging   smooth-running   spring in the lake bottom
how its refluxes collide   intertwine
like superimposed vinyl records
that tease out lingering sorrows   the past and present

the world has many lakes
some frozen   some boiling at a volcano's peak
some saltier than seawater
most fresh and cool, green and pleasing

stillness is self weighing on self
many things controlled unwittingly

断水

如果不把刀拔上来
水就断着
一直不拔上来
就一直断
再插深一点
就在深处断
直插到底
刀刃埋进坚硬的河床
那握刀的手就可以离开
水面就越没有动静

Broken Water

if the knife isn't pulled up
water will break
if still not pulled up
water will keep breaking
if tucked in deeper
water will break deeper
tucked in all the way
the knife sinks into the hard riverbed
the hand gripping it can leave now
the water surface no longer bears movement

心窝

你是嵌在世界中的
像一座山里埋着岩石
岩石里隐着窨罅
里面穿流着腐蚀性的水
一座山的强硬肉身
也可能有松动的时候
一个心窝
有一天会塌毁

Pit of the Stomach

you are lodged in the center of the world
like a rock buried in a mountain
holes and fissures are hidden in the rock
corrosive water flowing inside
a mountain's hard flesh
may loosen up too
the pit of the stomach
will collapse one day

一个胸腔的力量太小

痛是一座大橱　大柜　大屋　大殿
有无数的隔层　抽屉　房间　门　窗　洞
全上了封条

痛是车水马龙的十字路口
卡车　小车　摩托车　三轮车　自行车
横来竖去　堵了
警车的红灯从烟雾里烧过来

痛是正在施工的大工地
打砖机　切割机　冲击钻　钢锯　电焊　钉　锤
齐上阵

痛得这样彻底却还没到底
痛得这样细密却没有痛透
痛得这样庞大却还在围困中
痛得这样繁杂喧闹却没有一点声音
痛得即断即裂即碎却坚如磐石

一个胸腔的力量太小
不够用于痛
用于痛的风暴　战争　大野大天
把旗帜插在
火山般爆发的心尖

The Power of a Chest Cavity Is Too Weak

pain is a big wardrobe   cabinet   house   temple hall
with countless layers   drawers   rooms   doors   windows   holes
all sealed

pain is the crossroad of heavy traffic
trucks   cars   motorcycles   rickshaws   bicycles
in a chaos   blocked
red lights of a police car burn across a fog of smoke

pain is a large construction site in progress
cement brick machines   cutting machines   drills   hacksaws
      electric welders   nails   hammers
all in battle

pain so utter yet endless
so dense yet limited
so vast yet besieged
so noisy yet soundless
so shattered yet firm like a rock

the power of a chest cavity is too weak
not enough for pain
or its storm   war   vast wild and sky
it can't plant a flag
at the exploding peak of the volcano's heart

不能使痛

回到小路　故乡

回到山崖边的鸟巢

can't make pain

return to a path   to hometown

return to a nest near the cliff

世界的心总是隐隐的疼

在层层喧哗和纷乱之下
有一根筋在红肿颤动
弥漫向旁边的支脉　深入
基石　墙　一个个房间
梦的过道　鸟儿的心　花朵的香
它的联系越来越广大深远了
再无法拔取出来
世界的心总是隐隐的疼

The World's Heart Always Aches Faintly

beneath layers of clamor and turmoil
an inflamed tendon trembles
it spreads to branches nearby   deep into
cornerstones   walls   room by room
dream corridors   bird hearts   floral scents
its nexuses expand and reach further
they can never be extracted
the world's heart always aches faintly

繁星呈现

很多的话越来越离心
很多的诗越来越掏空真情
万吨语言不如一次真实的日出
一次真实的日出
不如心头流不出的一滴血

黑暗重进黑暗
黑暗无底
繁星呈现

Many Stars Emerge

more and more words deviate from the heart
more and more poems empty out true feelings
ten thousand tons of language can't match a real sunrise
a real sunrise
can't match a drop of blood the heart can't shed

black reenters black
black is endless
many stars emerge

有一天会彻底停顿下来

你左边的胸膛里有一只小船
有时它剧烈颠荡起来　扯动手臂和后背的纤缆
拖出大小血管里的风暴
肩胛骨像岬角　雪浪碎裂又碎裂

你用一只手掌按住它　再重叠上另一只
像一个盖子加上一块石头
还要气息咻咻地劝慰　好了　别这样　上帝已经知道

它会慢慢平复　纹丝不动地夹在里面
敏感的　不能有一点点风溜进去

有一天会彻底停顿下来
大海上的船只正乘风破浪

One Day It Will Stop Completely

there is a small boat in your left chest
sometimes it rocks violently   jerking fibers in arms and back
dragging storms out of big and small blood vessels
shoulder blade like a cape   where white waves break and break

you press it with one palm   then with the other
like placing a rock on a lid
and consoling it breathlessly   *please   don't   God already knows*

it will calm down   firmly stuck inside
sensibly   with no wind sneaking in

one day it will stop completely
boats at sea are riding on waves and wind

那束白花

那束白花
怎么这么白

那束白花
其实不怎么白

只因为那一刻
白到白的底线

白在黑上

That Bouquet of White Flowers

that bouquet of white flowers
why so white

that bouquet of white flowers
isn't that white

just because at that instant
white was white's bottom line

white above black

话剧的空间

字　词　停顿——
一条山溪　一道峻岭　一座寺院
从远方到了近前
深渊吊挂在空中　各个方向都能看见
一朵浪花　在汪洋跪拜
群峰埋在海底

蓝天从骨节里出来
脚掌吸起大地的寂静
刀子　绳索　针　碎刃　从心间过
广场　大街　医院　监狱　封闭的梦
在脑际里穿
带动古老的欢乐和山高水长

悲哀耸立　白色麻衣拂动宽大的皱褶
连接滚滚的风

平台　梯级　墙　红日　月亮　星河
可以推倒　重构
新的混沌
等待一个雪亮的裂口
一个木偶流出泪水

一小时不止一万年
场灯亮起来了　谢幕
观众
还没有亮起来

Space of Drama

word   phrase   period—
a mountain stream   a lofty mountain range   a monastery
from far to near
abyss hangs in mid-sky   visible in all directions
a wave   kowtows before the ocean
mountain peaks buried under the sea

a blue sky emerges from bone joints
soles breathe the stillness of the universe
knife   rope   needle   blade fragments   through the heart
square   avenue   hospital   jail   sealed dream
weaving through thoughts
spurring ancient joys and high mountains high waters

towering sorrow   white linen swishing wide creases
connecting tides of wind

platform   stairs   wall   sun   moon   Milky Way
can be toppled   and rebuilt
a new chaos
waiting for a shiny crack
a puppet sheds tears

an hour exceeds ten thousand years
the hall lights up   curtain call
spectators
yet luminous

独舞

积压成石头的风暴
放出来
有方的　扁的　多边形的
太重了
落到地上
滚到沟里　池塘里　埋入淤泥

大水必须不动
顶它的是一根细柱子

春花在盖好香气后再张嘴
等待去年和前年的蝴蝶

每跟骨头准备好弯曲
经络预备着缠绕
激流撞向绝壁不许碎开

来不及弥合的虚空
让闪电去填充

水晶的心
提一个陨石
一大群的光在啃

Solo Dance

storms backlogged into rocks
free themselves
square   flat   polygonal
too heavy
fall to the ground
tumble into a ditch   a pond   buried in silt

held by a thin pillar
grand water must be still

aroma bottled up, spring flowers open their mouths
waiting for butterflies of years past

each bone ready to bend
meridians to meander
torrent against a steep must not break

too late to heal the void
let lightning seal it

crystal heart
holds a meteorite
bitten by a large band of light

道路联向天边
视线收到近前
一个小碗

黑是黑的黑布袋
一视同仁

roads link to sky's edge
vision draws close
a small bowl

black is darkness in a black cloth sack
all seen as the same

只有太阳能做太阳的事情

绵长的小道　绕过山腰
拦住起起伏伏的松涛

也只有太阳能照顾得过来
使每一根松针变成光芒
使每一蓬松针变成光芒
无穷无尽的光芒汇成光海
山道成了光的岸
你成了光之岸的人

也只有太阳
全部的功能就是发光
也只有太阳
能做太阳的事情

Only the Sun Can Do What the Sun Does

a long and winding path   around a mountainside
blocks off a wavy wind in the pines

only the sun can take care of these
transforming each pine needle into radiance
each cluster of pine needles into radiance
the infinite radiance swells into a sea of light
the mountain path becomes a shore of light
you become a man on the shore of light

only the sun
has a full function of radiating light
only the sun
can do what the sun does

与梁野山瀑布群

何处来
一群群透明的小精灵　急急地跑
撞到一起了　再分开　又多出一些小队伍
是谁牵了谁的手　脚丫子踩了脚丫子
挤成一堆堆　一窝窝　嘻嘻哈哈
你推我　我推你
集体蹦极

拽成竖弦千万丝　飘飞的音符满山野
却不告诉我　大山的腹腔
是怎样的迷宫
多少洞中洞　罅中罅　一条缝的小门重重
锁细脖子　捏小身子
钻出簧管笛孔排排　曲韵庞杂在岩层之下
直到在不经意间
被天光炫得睁不开眼

针秒站不稳在片刻不停里
思想碰不进无旁顾的表情
一座山　要构筑怎样的交响

沿着你　我是一只最笨的猴子
把石头当可靠的朋友　容我全身重量的蹬踢
藤条和树枝是救助的手　把我提上去

With Mount Liangye Falls

from nowhere
groups of transparent elves   run in a flurry
collide together   then separate   more little troupes emerge
who is tugging at whose hand   this foot is stepping on that foot
squeezed into piles   into nests   *hehe haha*
you push me   I push you
a mass bungee jumping

thousands of vertical strings are swaying   notes fly over mountains
     and fields
yet they do not say   what labyrinth
is the mountain's belly
O many caves in caves   gaps in gaps   doors over doors in a crack
necks thinly sucked in   bodies squeezed smaller
rows of reed pipes and flute holes   melodies jumbled beneath the strata
until inadvertently
dazzled by skylight eyes can't open

seconds can't stand firmly within continuity
thoughts can't penetrate a focused expression
what symphony   does a mountain want to build

trailing along you   I am the most foolish monkey
who treats the stone as a reliable friend   allowing my body to kick
     at random
canes and branches are helping hands   they pull me up

我仅有的力气被拔得越来越细了
还够不着你的万分之一

有多少的不可企及深不可测
我必须借助更繁复的配置
打通和扩建自己

想着你
范围之外　　还有阶梯

my only strength is thinning out
and can't even reach the slightest of you

O many unreachables, unfathomables
I must use a more complex installation
to break open myself and expand

thinking of you
beyond the confines   there are still flights of steps

两座白色房子

在道山路
我的目光停留在
一座白色房子上
十二年前
我的女儿出生在里面
那一天在那座房子里
一共出生了三十九个婴儿

那一天的前一天　再前一天　再前一天……
那一天的后一天　再后一天　再后一天……
一共出生了多少婴儿……

妇女们把十月怀胎的身体放进去
不久就有一个孩子抱出来
这么重要的一座房子　人们视而不见

我同时想到近郊处的一座白色房子
想着从这座房子出来的人多少年后都会进入那座白色房子
都要躺在冰冷的铁床上进入炉火涅槃成气体　烟尘

这么重要的一座房子
人们在送过亲人　朋友　叹息　欷歔之后
头也不回地走了
好像再与它无关

Two White Houses

at Daoshan Road
my gaze dwells
on a white house
where my daughter was born
twelve years ago
on that day
thirty-nine babies were born there

the day before that day   two days before   three days before . . .
the day after that day   two days later   three days later . . .
how many babies were born . . .

women arrive in their pregnant bodies of ten months
and leave with each a baby in her arms
such a crucial house   we turn a blind eye to it

I think of another white house in the suburbs
and those who leave the first white house only to enter the other
        years later
lying on an icy iron bed to enter a stove where nirvana is air   smoke
        and dust

such a crucial house
they send off their kin and friends   sigh   sob
and leave without looking back
as if they had nothing to do with it

让你看人间的繁星灿烂

那个打手机的人
眼睛里有一个狂喜

那只俯冲而过的大鸟
胸膛里有一个狂喜

那盆盛开的太阳花
每一个心蕊都是一个狂喜

那玉兰树顶的嫩叶抖了抖
一定有狂喜　从很深的根里涌上去

那闷头赶路的大货车
压抑着一个狂喜
等着到达目的地时释放出来

那接到录取通知单的女孩
紧抱着一个狂喜
急不可耐地要爆炸开

我得一个个记下来
说不定哪天　我也有一个
也拿去和它们放在一起

我还会记下更多　更多
让你看人间的繁星灿烂
让你也有一个狂喜

May You See the Splendor of Stars in This World

the man on the cellphone
has a euphoria in his eyes

the big bird plunging down
has a euphoria in its chest

the pot of sunflowers in full bloom
has a euphoria at the heart of each petal

the magnolia treetop shakes its tender leaves
there must be a euphoria   gushing up from roots deep down

the truck buries its head and rushes its way
suppresses a euphoria
waiting to free it at its destination

the girl who has received her acceptance letter
tightly hugs a euphoria
that can't wait to explode

I must record them one by one
who knows which day   I'd have one
to put together with the rest

I will record more   more
so you may see the splendor of stars in this world
may you too have a euphoria

YI LU (伊路) is a theater scenographer who leads a parallel life as a poet. Born in 1956, she is the author of five books of poetry, including the award-winning titles, *See* (2004) and *Using Two Seas* (2009). Her fifth volume, *Forever Lingering* (2011), was published by Culture and Art Press in Beijing. Yi is known for her elegant and distilled lyrical voice, as well as her ecological awareness. Her honors include the Hundred Flowers Award for Literature and other distinguished literary prizes from Fujian province. A theatrical stage and set designer at the People's Art Theatre in Fujian, she lives in the southern coastal city of Fuzhou.

MELISSA KWASNY is the author of five books of poems, including, most recently, *Pictograph* (2015), *The Nine Senses* (2011), and *Reading Novalis in Montana* (2009), all from Milkweed Editions. Her book of essays, *Earth Recitals: Essays on Image and Vision*, was published by Lynx House Press in 2013. She lives in the Elkhorn Mountains of western Montana.

FIONA SZE-LORRAIN writes and translates in English, French, and Chinese. Her new poetry collection, *The Ruined Elegance* (2016), will be published by Princeton University Press in the Princeton Series of Contemporary Poets. The author of two previous titles, *My Funeral Gondola* (2013) and *Water the Moon* (2010), as well as several translations of contemporary Chinese, French, and American poets, she is a *zheng* harpist and an editor at Vif Éditions. She lives in Paris, France.